Endless Knot
佛教的生命、生死、生活學

Endless Knot

Venerable Master Hsing Yun
on Living, Dying, and Learning

Venerable Master Hsing Yun

Buddha's Light Publishing, Los Angeles

© 2012 Buddha's Light Publishing
First Edition

By Venerable Master Hsing Yun
Edited by Nathan Michon and John Gill
Book designed by Wan Kah Ong
Cover photograph by Mario Cee

Published by Buddha's Light Publishing
3456 S. Glenmark Drive,
Hacienda Heights, CA 91745, U.S.A.
Tel: (626) 923-5144
Fax: (626) 923-5145
E-mail: itc@blia.org
Website: www.blpusa.com

Printed in Taiwan.

Library of Congress Cataloging-in-Publication Data

Xingyun, 1927-
   Endless knot : Venerable Master Hsing Yun on living, dying, and learning / Venerable Master Hsing Yun. — First Edition.
      pages cm
   Translated and edited by Fo Guang Shan International Translation Center.

   ISBN 978-1-932293-71-5
   1. Religious life—Buddhism. I. Title.

   BQ9800.F6392X55428 2013
   294.3'92—dc23

                              2012033199

Contents

Acknowledgments

Like all of Buddha's Light Publishing's endeavors, this project benefited from the contributions of many people. We would like to thank Venerable Tzu Jung, the Chief Executive of the Fo Guang Shan International Translation Center (FGSITC), Venerble Hui Chi, Abbot of Hsi Lai Temple, and Venerable Yi Chao, Director of FGSITC for their support and leadership.

Guangjian Hou, Sheley Lee, Gena Yu, and Amanda Ling provided the translation. Nathan Michon and John Gill collected and edited the texts, and Louvenia Ortega proofread the manuscript and prepared it for publication. The book was designed by Wan Kah Ong, the cover was designed by John Gill, and Mario Cee provided the cover photographs. Our appreciation goes to everyone who supported this project from conception to completion.

Part I

Understanding Life

The mind is large beyond comparison. If we were to try and quantify it, we could say it is as vast as the emptiness of the universe, or even larger. In the Buddhist sutras it is said that "the mind can encompass all of space, with worlds as numerous as the sands of the Ganges." If each of us can encompass the universe with our minds, then surely a single person can accomplish great things. This is the essence of the mind: it is life itself, and it is because of life that all things have purpose.

> If each of us can encompass the universe with our minds, then surely a single person can accomplish great things.

According to the Buddhist text the *Treatise on the Awakening of Faith in Mahayana*, the mind has three great qualities: the mind's essence, already mentioned, as well as the mind's form and the mind's function.

The mind of every being possesses an essence that continues from birth to death and on to the next life. However, the mind also possesses a form that changes throughout life's various stages, from birth to death and from death to birth. The mind's function is the act of living—all the things that we do throughout our existence. In this world the past, present, and future all reside in the mind, and all internal and external phenomena are products of consciousness. Consciousness itself is but a function of the mind.

Human beings have an essence, form, and function as well. Life is the essence of human beings, the cycle of birth and death is our form, and living is our function. This is the Buddhist view of our human world, and how I will continue to discuss life and death in this book. Let us start first with the essence, life itself.

> Life is the essence of human beings, the cycle of birth and death is our form, and living is our function.

In this perspective of life, everything is a part of life and we all actively participate in life. Life gives us purpose. Life is the most precious and valuable thing on earth. Life is moving, growing, and constructive. If we do not express life's function in our day to day existence, then our lives will lack vitality.

People have lives so they can move and laugh, so they can experience joy, anger, sadness, and happiness. The birds flying in the sky, the fish swimming in the sea, the leopards in the mountains, and the house cats and dogs all have life. If we expand our understanding of life, then the sun, moon and stars as well as the earth that we live on all have life. The flowers, grass, trees, tables, chairs, houses, and clothes all have life. If you cherish a garment, it can last one or two decades, whereas if you don't cherish it, it can be ruined in a matter of months. So if you love life, you can live a long time. In order to cherish life, we must appreciate everything that we have, because only then are we able to sustain our lives and all the life around us.

> People do not exist alone. The world and universe have one giant life - it lives and shares the same body.

People do not exist alone. The world and universe have one giant life—it lives and shares the same body. Life is not something we experience by ourselves. Without a father or mother, I could not have been born. Life is about coexistence. Without help from others, I can't go on living. We must recognize that and live together so that humanity can have peace. We must coexist for the world to not just continue, but continue in the utmost auspiciousness and to see the full potential of what this experience of life has to offer.

Life needs many causes and conditions to exist. We need our parents to take care of us at birth. We need farmers, workers, merchants, and others to provide food and various items for us. Without them, we cannot sustain our lives. Life is completely interrelated. If a seed were placed on a table or floor, it would not grow. It needs the conditions of soil, water, sunlight, and air for it to flower and bear fruit. People, likewise, cannot just randomly appear in the world from nowhere. Besides other conditions, we are born relying on love. Only because the parents' causes and conditions brought them together does the individual come to be. The four great elements of earth, water, fire, and wind are all part of life. We have the solidity of earth, the liquidity of water, the heat of fire and the movement of wind. Without sunlight, the trees, and flowers cannot mature. Without the nourishment of water, nothing can grow. Therefore, life's meaning must also have the causes and conditions of various elements propelling it to thrive. What appears to be our "self" is actually limitless, and as such we should mutually benefit one another so we can all have a prosperous life.

In human life, we survive because of the causes and conditions provided by so many others in this web of life. I should therefore help contribute to their sustenance. In everyday life, we should constantly do things to inspire people and we should be appreciative of what others do for us. If love for all existence can grow in our lives, our lives become truly meaningful.

> We survive because of the causes and conditions provided by so many others in this web of life. I should therefore help contribute to their sustenance.

Life is like a string of prayer beads. A life does not disappear; lives are strung together—birth begets death and death

5

begets birth; therefore, death means rebirth. There is endless living and dying, dying and living. Life is impermanent, but impermanence is not to be feared. Impermanence is a type of metamorphosis: like the movement on a clock, life ultimately returns to the starting point.

In this lifetime, in the limitless incalculably long stream of life, we are only at one of the stops. Thus, we can't view this one lifetime as our entire life. Don't be too happy if you are living a good life, because it will change. If you are not living a good life, don't despair, because that too can be changed. The meaning of life is to create life and provide others with the causes and conditions to live good lives. We must support others, for we gain many benefits from them.

The meaning of life is to create life and provide others with the causes and conditions to live good lives.

HOW DID WE GET HERE?

What does life look like? This life is filled with men, women, intelligence, stupidity, beauty, ugliness, strength, and weakness. In order to accommodate life, we need to understand the past, present, and the future. In Buddhism, we have a saying:

"Come to know the karma of your past life by seeing what befalls you in this life." From the good fortune in this life, we can understand the karma we created in past lives. This is similar to how, when a flower blooms, whether it is beautiful or not is related to its fertilizer and seed.

In the same way, Buddhism also says, "Come to know your future outcome by looking at what you are doing now." The karma we create in this lifetime will bear fruit in the future. Buddhism addresses the three time periods—past, present, and future. People often ask, "Where does life come from?" We cannot say where life comes from. In Buddhism we think that life is cyclical rather than linear. Life is not from point A to point B, nor does it have a beginning and an end.

> Life is cyclical rather than linear, life is not from point A to point B, nor does it have a beginning and an end.

Life is like spring, summer, fall and winter. Once winter arrives, is spring far behind? There is birth, old age, sickness and death. After death, comes birth. So when there is birth, it is not entirely joyful because one day there will be death. On the other hand, when there is death, it is not entirely sorrowful. The body has become like an old, rusty car that eventually goes to the junkyard. After death, one will be reborn into a new body. This world has arising, abiding, change, and cessation.

Another example would be a new house that falls into ruin after many years; it will need to be torn down and reconstructed. Within the mind is the arising, abiding, change, and cessation of all existence. Our thoughts constantly arise and cease, and then arise again. It's like the clock we mentioned earlier, after it gets to twelve o'clock, it starts again.

The Buddha taught the "twelve links of dependent origination," which describes where people come from. Where do people come from? People come from ignorance. Ignorance is being unclear about and not knowing the principles of life. Why do people not know it? When people come to the present life from the previous life, there is the intermediate state of transmission. After changing from one body, people become confused so it is difficult to know what has happened in a previous life. When one dies in the present life, we'll change into another body in the next life and become confused once again.

> Where do people come from? People come from ignorance. Ignorance is being unclear about and not knowing the principles of life.

Even though there is ignorance, there is still a cycle through births and deaths through which the mind flows. It is because of ignorance that the mind flows through the cycle of birth and death. From as much as a single thought of ignorance all good

and bad actions arise, and from these past actions consciousness arises.

Consciousness is a function of
the mind that allows one to distin-
guish phenomena. When a mother
and father come together and the
mother becomes pregnant, consciousness and body come together
and the sense organs begin to develop. For instance, through the newly
developing eyes there is a visual
sense, able to differentiate various

**With distinction
of phenomena,
the distinction
between painful
and pleasurable
feeling arises.
From these
feelings, craving
arises.**

colors like red, yellow, blue, white and black. The ears can differentiate among various sounds, and the body can sense temperature. With this distinction of phenomena, the distinction
between painful and pleasurable feeling arises. From these feelings, craving arises. Craving causes us to be stubborn towards
what we like, thinking, "If I like it, I must get it, if I don't like
it, I will avoid it." This attitude results in us generating karma
that will revisit us in the future, which causes us to continue in
the cycle of birth and death.

From the past to the present, and from the present to the
future, we need to clarify the path as it is not easy to understand. The path, put simply, is cause, condition, and effect. Life
cycles around due to cause, condition and effect. Often people

will talk about cause and effect, but within cause and effect conditions are also present. If there are no causes and no conditions, there will be no effect. Suppose you had a father but no mother—you would not be able to be born. With only a mother but no father, we cannot be born so we need both a father and mother as our conditions.

People all have desires that bring forth the force of life. Impermanence also allows our lives to continue, expand, and have power. How can we understand the impermanence of life? It is like how a girl is called a "baby girl" at birth but as she grows, she is called a "little girl." Once she is in school, she is called a "school girl" followed by "miss," "mother," and "old woman" as she ages. So which stage is really her? Is it the baby girl, the school girl, or the old woman? Actually these are all part of the many changes of life. The impermanence of life also brings life and death. But there is no need to be too concerned; relax and be comfortable, taking each stage as it comes. Just have faith in the process, because life doesn't perish.

In Christianity, it is said that "Faith is eternal." This is true: the lives of the faithful will go on endlessly, but the lives of

> Impermanence allows our lives to continue, expand, and have power. The impermanence of life also brings life and death.

those who are not faithful will not be cut off. It is only the body that dies. Don't be too worried. Treasure your life and let things take their course. Accept all types of change and all types of pressure.

I often wish that with just this body of mine, with this single life and mind, that I can diligently expand my life to encompass the whole world, like a drop of water following the current into the ocean until it expands into the limitless beyond. Just as a single drop of water helps a plant to grow beautifully, so too can something as small as one person's life blend into a county, a culture, even the whole universe until all existence is one. This is the essence of a life of coexistence.

> Just as a single drop of water helps a plant to grow beautifully, so too can something as small as one person's life blend into a county, a culture, even the whole universe. until all existence is one.

How to Nurture Life

How to sustain life is easy to understand. For example, when we eat, it's for sustaining life, to continue living. We wear clothes to keep our bodies healthy and not catch a cold. We need to live in an environment that is peaceful and sanitary in order to avoid disease and contagions. Riding in a car or boat or flying in a plane are all efforts to save time since time is life. Emotions, entertainment, exercise, and medical care are all ways to sustain and to extend life.

There are many causes that maintain life in the universe. For instance, faith can also sustain our life. Some say, "People still die even with religious beliefs!" Of course people still die with religious beliefs, but the situation is different. Some people die with terror, some die with a peaceful smile, and then there are others who cannot withstand any adversity and wish to die. Some learn to endure and others understand living is not just for oneself but also for one's parents and family, or even others throughout the world.

There is one forest in Japan where people go to commit suicide. Some people who are at wits end will go into the forest to commit suicide. There is a plaque at the entrance of the forest that says "Please think about your family, parents and children—stay out of the forest! There are many causes in life that you must not ignore. Reconsider everything and think it through."

Religion and faith give us ideals that ask us to not only think about

Religion and faith give us ideals that ask us to not only think about ourselves, but to think about the welfare of others.

ourselves, but to think about the welfare of others. We should think about being compassionate, wise, and having a passion for life. For example, one can always do volunteer work and serve the community. Helping others is the key to happiness. We need to broadcast the joy in our lives. With this mindset, it would not be easy to end one's life.

We can continue to live our life because everyone protects it. Thus, we cannot casually waste life. Faith is having something to hold onto. For example, when there is a problem, we can ask our parents for guidance. Between husbands and wives, there is another party to consult with. We can even ask our children and friends for their opinions since we are all connected to each other. Faith can give us the strength to live and provide hope for the future. It lets us believe that our present suffering will change one day. With faith, even while encountering difficulties, adversity or advanced age and disease, we'll know how that reality can change. With faith we can believe in our own strength, and in our own passion to make life better.

In addition to having a physical life, and emotional life, and a community life, we also need to have a life of faith. Some say "I don't believe in any of that." If you don't have faith, then you don't have anything! With faith, it's like having a bridge when you need to cross the river, or a ferry that can safely get you across. Even with worries, there is no fear since there is the bridge and ferry of faith that can help you overcome your difficulties. Maybe you'll think "one needs to rely on oneself for life." But with age and immobility one needs crutches. With disease, we must rely on doctors and nurses for treatment. So our lives are intertwined. Everyone needs me and I need everyone.

◎◎ ◎◎ ◎◎

THE ORIGIN OF LIFE

Where does life come from? Anthropologists say life comes from parents. Where do parents come from? They come from our grandparents, and grandparents come from great grandparents. One might ask, "Well, who are our earliest ancestors?" Some say people evolved from primates, but where do primates come from? Primates evolved from amoebas. Well, where do amoebas come from? Ultimately it's hard to explain clearly. It's just like Indian religions saying that people originated from Brahma. Some come from Brahma's eyes, some from his mouth, and some from his belly button, each resulting in a different kind of person. But then where does Brahma come from? It remains an unanswered question. Christians say God created man. But then where does God come from? It's yet another unanswered question.

Daoism says that everything comes from *yin* and *yang*. But then where do *yin* and *yang* come from? Regardless of evolution or other explanations, we still don't know the ultimate origins of human beings.

Why? Because people don't come from one place. People come because of each other. The Three Treatise School, one of the great philosophical schools of Buddhism, says "When this is present, that comes to be; when this is absent, that does not come to be." There is no answer to the question of which came first, the chicken or the egg. If the chicken came first, and there was no egg, then where did the chicken come from? If the egg was first, with no chicken before it, then how did the egg come about? So where do people come from? In Buddhism, all things come from love, because of love from the parents. Life comes from the union of the body and karma.

"When this is present, that comes to be; when this is absent, that does not come to be."

But where do I really come from? In Buddhism this is related to the question "Who am I?" or "What is the real me?" There is a story both slightly gruesome and silly in the sutras in which a lone traveler wasn't able to find lodging. He ended up sleeping in the shrine of a local folk deity on the outskirts of town, but just as he started to fall asleep under the altar, he noticed a small creature carrying a corpse. The frightened traveler exclaimed, "Oh no, I see a demon!"

As he was stricken with fear, a larger demon came and scared the traveler even more. The two demons began arguing. The larger demon asked the smaller demon, "Why did you carry my corpse here?"

The smaller demon answered, "This is my corpse! How can you say it's yours?" As the two argued back and forth, the traveler witnessed it all and broke out in a cold sweat. The smaller demon said, "Hey, there's a human. Don't be afraid, come and help us confirm who this corpse belongs to."

The traveler thought to himself, "Even though I saw the smaller one carry the corpse here, if I say that, the big one will be upset. But I cannot lie! Oh no! It looks like I won't be able to escape today."

The traveler decided to tell the truth and said, "This body belongs to the smaller demon." The larger demon was furious upon hearing this, ripped off the traveler's right arm, and ate it with a loud crunch. The smaller demon took a look and thought, "Oh no! The traveler spoke out for me and had his right arm eaten off, what am I going to do? Oh, look, there is the right arm on the corpse."

The smaller demon took the right arm from the corpse and attached it to the traveler's body. But the larger demon wouldn't give up and also ate the traveler's left arm. The smaller demon took the left arm of the corpse and attached it to the traveler. In the end, the traveler's limbs were all eaten and replaced with those of the corpse's body, much like a kidney, heart or other organ transplant.

After the two demons finished their misdeeds, they vanished into thin air, leaving the traveler mumbling to himself, "Who am I? Once I was me, but not anymore. Whose body is this?" Then he had a realization: This body is not mine. Whether it is male or female, old or young, beautiful or ugly, this outer body will die one day. It will not be mine after it is dead. Not only can I not take any of my worldly possessions, but not even this body will follow me. All I will take into the next life is my karma.

Not only can I not take all my worldly possessions, but not even this body will follow me. All I will take into the next life is my karma.

Where do people come from? Where do the dead go? There is a Chinese poem that reads: "For sentient beings, to be reborn is suffering. The grandson marries the grandmother, the livestock sit at the table, and the family gets cooked in the pots." This means that there is a family where the grandson is getting married. Who is the bride? It's the grandmother who has died and been reborn. The livestock raised in another life have become friends and family in this life. The family of a previous life is now being cooked in the pot. So the cycle of birth and death can be scary. Our future depends on how we act in this life. It's like having plenty of wealth in your home country, even if you emigrate abroad and come back, you still have a chance. If you spend it all, there is little for you to use upon your return. It is best to buy an umbrella on a clear day before the clouds come. You should prepare a flashlight beforehand, so that you will have it when darkness arrives.

Where does life come from? The fact is that it's not necessary to know all the specific details. Everyone's karma and conditions are complex; we could keep asking questions forever to go back further and further. Rather than spending so much of our time and energy focusing on the past, what is actually important is preparing for the future. Spring is for sowing seeds of good deeds so that they can be harvested in the fall. So how does one sow seeds in life? Society is our field. The wise, the sagely, the skillful, and the benevolent are our field of merit. The Buddha and our parents are our field of respect. The poor and suffering are our field of compassion. We can sow seeds among them. There should be no worries if you sow seeds abundantly.

> Rather than spending so much of our time and energy focusing on the past, what is actually important is preparing for the future.

THE IMPERMANENCE OF LIFE

The essence of life does not change, though the form of life is always changing. Transsexuals can even change their gender, so why can being rich or poor not change? Buddhism calls this "impermanence," and the forces of impermanence are always at play. Good things will come to an end if they are not preserved. Bad things can be remedied to become good things. I am poor, but with hard work, I will find a way. I am dumb, but if I read a lot I can eventually become a little smarter.

> The essence of life does not change, though the form of life is always changing. Buddhism calls this "impermanence," and the forces of impermanence are always at play.

In my childhood, my family was very poor and didn't have money for me to go to school. What can a seven or eight year old child do? When the adults went out, I was left home alone. All I could do was clean the house. To heat the house, we burned logs and grass. After a little while, the fire was no longer bright. Hence, I would clean the ashes so that the fire would burn brighter when the adults got home.

19

Due to my family's poverty, we often only ate breakfast and weren't sure whether we'd have lunch or dinner. Seeing the consternation in the adults at this predicament, and not being old enough to do anything else, I would go outside to collect nails and sell them for a few cents. I collected flower blossoms to sell at the medical shop and I even collected dog droppings to sell as manure. At that young age, I still figured out ways to help my family. I was diligent and committed myself to finding ways to do what I could for my family. When they didn't have money to buy groceries or didn't have anything to eat, I would proudly take out a few coins and buy food for the family.

In addition, my family would only feed the dog once a day at night, which felt so inhumane! So if there was any food in the house, I would secretly give it to the dog when no one else was around. Sometimes, I would give candy to the neighbor's kids. I felt that I'd find a way in the future. Why? Because I try to be a caring person. Even though my family was very poor, there would be change.

Even after I became a monk, my teacher would scold me, discipline me, and force me into a life that felt inhuman. But I thought to myself, "This will change, because I am in the learning stage." As I grew over the next few years there were always changes, so I recognized that life was impermanent. People need not fear change. Have faith and a compassionate heart because everything can be changed.

In this world, sometimes a clear day can suddenly turn rainy. This isn't necessarily bad. The trees and flowers need the water's nourishment. If it rained daily but suddenly became sunny, that would be good too. With the sun shining bright, it's more convenient to do things. It's like a caterpillar needing change in order to become a beautiful butterfly. Change provides the opportunities we need to grow and flourish.

> It's like a caterpillar needing change in order to become a beautiful butterfly. Change provides the opportunities we need to grow and flourish.

Many years ago, a wealthy devotee encouraged me to set up a college. He said he would donate 50 million New Taiwan Dollars. I said, "I can't accept your money, since the Ministry of Education has not allowed us to set up a college. When we are ready to set up the college, though, we'll come to you."

He said, "No, while I have the money now, you just take the $50 million NT because this money won't always be mine. When I no longer have the money, even if you ask me for it, I cannot give it to you."

Life is ever-changing. As long as you use your intelligence, use your heart, and follow changes as they occur, things can just change for the better without getting worse. If you want to become smarter, you need to make more of an effort, and to become rich, you'll need to work harder. Life has limitless energy and limitless treasures.

Maybe you feel that life is not fair in this world and you are often wronged. But you are able to face any adversity if you cultivate a peaceful heart. Perhaps you feel that you don't have good affinities, and that wealth and fortune belong only to others. Perhaps you had some good karma and were about to earn a large amount of money, but at the last minute, everything fell apart. Things change, but it's alright because this just means that the conditions have not yet come to fruition. In this life, if you are poor then take action to change your conditions as best as you can. This will show that you can pass any obstacles. Change is actually not scary at all. The only scary thing would be if there was no change.

> Change is actually not scary at all. The only scary thing would be if there was no change.

In order to develop the strength and will to live, many plants need only a tiny crack to grow, even on a cement road. Even a little flower on the wall shows its beauty flowing in the wind. As long as we develop our own strength to live, there is no need to fear the constant changes in life. Following the constant change will make life more beautiful.

COEXISTENCE

Lives are all interrelated. There was a general in the past who wanted to control a city and told his soldiers "If you can defeat this city you will be rewarded handsomely, and receive whatever you desire."

The troops seized the entire city and killed everyone to get their reward. When the general asked the troops what they wanted, they responded, "We want liquor!"

The general said, "Here's some money, go buy your liquor."

The general asked what else the troops wanted.

The troops yelled back, "Women!"

The general said, "No problem, go to the city and take your pick."

The troops were celebrating, but when they went to the city, they found that all the stores were destroyed. No one was selling liquor and there were no women. They had killed the entire city, destroyed all its goods, and cut off all their supplies. It was only then that they realized their victory was in fact defeat.

When the Fo Guang Shan Pumen Middle School girl's basketball team competed against students from Daye College we told them, "You must have mutual respect and cannot see the other team as the enemy. Even if they are the opposing team, we cannot play without them, so you need to protect your competitor." Life is mutually beneficial: I am part of you, and you are part of me. Mutual respect and mutual acceptance is like the Chinese saying "Heroes cherish heroes." This means that heroes are those who mutually respect and love each other. It may appear they are only helping others but, in truth, everyone benefits through such cooperation.

Life is mutually beneficial: I am part of you, and you are part of me.

Life is equal at its essence, without any differentiation between the high and the low. Some people perceive the politically powerful as superior, while the average citizen is disregarded in any critical discussion. However, political leaders are also often called "public servants." The people are the masters! So I feel that life is mutually sustained. It's like an election: if no citizen casts a vote, how can there be elected officials? If you happen to attain a high position, it is important not to feel that you are too great.

Life is equal at its essence, without any differentiation between the high and the low.

There was a teacher whose wedding I officiated. Time flew by and ten years passed. He had kids and said it was hard to be a parent. When having dinner at home, the kids would complain about the food not tasting good. They would argue and complain and made things very difficult for the parents and the parents couldn't stand it.

I told him, "Go back to your kids and say, 'Your father is useless and unable to earn a lot of money. I'm unable to buy nice food for you to eat. I'm so sorry!'"

The teacher did just as I told him. Upon hearing that, the children quickly said, "Father, don't worry, you're wonderful! The dishes are so tasty!"

The lesson of this story is that to just be wonderful is not quite enough. We must carry a modest, humble heart to live in harmony with others around us.

> We must carry a modest, humble heart to live in harmony with others around us.

I feel that Taiwan is a special place and not long ago a city on the southern side of the island, Kaohsiung, celebrated its eighty year anniversary. There was a heartfelt talk during which Kaohsiung mayor Xie Changting said, "When Kaohsiung was established, the population was only 40,000. Decades later, the population is at 500,000. We are all immigrants from various places."

When we really stop to think about it, all people on Earth are like immigrants, arriving from their previous lives into these current conditions and situations. So on what grounds can we discriminate against anyone?

Even if we are equal, we cannot all be exactly the same. We must have different functions in the world in order to work smoothly together. Imagine the eyes blaming the ears, "Why listen to what those people are saying? What's the point?"

The ears then blame the mouth, "Why are you still talking? Be quiet already!"

What could we accomplish by never listening and never talking? All the six sense organs need to coexist with each other or nothing in the body will function.

Within the five fingers, is there one that is better than the rest? Suppose the thumb yells out, "I'm number one!"

Then the index finger becomes upset and retorts, "I'm obviously more important. When I point the way, you all go along with me."

Then the middle finger, not to be outdone, stands up and says, "Maybe you all want to think you're the best, but of all fingers I'm clearly the longest and directly in the center. I'm the highest rank and you should all pay attention to me."

The ring finger, beginning to feel pushed out of place by the others, decides to get up and show off its jewelry. "Look, who's the most famous and who gets stared at the most? When people marry, all the gold and diamonds come to me. The opulence, the wealth, and the attention is all right here."

All the while the pinky finger was silent. Finally, one of the other fingers asked, "Why aren't you saying anything?"

The pinky was calm and collected, yet perfectly humble, in pointing out, "What can I say? Each of you is bigger, better, or richer than me. I am at the end and the smallest, so I can't even try to compete with you."

The other fingers, calmed by the pinky's modesty, paused to listen to what the pinky had to say. The pinky continued, "But when we join palms to pray or bow, I am closest to the Buddha, so it's not so bad being over here."

In the *Sutra of One Hundred Parables,* there is a story called "A Snake's Head and Tail." The tail hated that the head was always in the front, while the tail was always behind. The tail complained to the head, "You are always in the front and I am always in the back. If it weren't for me, how would you move around?" The tail then wrapped itself around a tree.

After a few days without any food, the head finally surrendered. "I don't want to be in front anymore, okay? I'm perfectly willing to follow. You can be the boss." Then the tail began to lead the way. But without any eyes to see the tail soon fell into a ditch and could not escape.

Life coexists. There is no need to reject anything. I feel that life is valuable, but what is even more valuable than life itself is the unity, peace, and harmony of that life. Everyone relies on each other and we must act in a way to support that existence.

⊙⊗⊙ ⊙⊗⊙ ⊙⊗⊙

LIFE AND THE NATURAL WORLD

The relationship between life and nature, between the elements, and between plant and animal life are all closely related. Non-vegetarians need animals to give up their lives to provide meat. Even though vegetarians only eat plants, if the plants were not alive and did not grow there would be no vegetables to eat. In the past, the Chinese worshipped the heavens that provided what mankind needed. People believed that we should be thankful, for we could not survive alone.

An organization in the United Nations once asked me, how can we protect the world's environment? I then recounted the Bodhisattva Shanzi story from the *Jatakas,* the stories of the Buddha's previous lives, to explain the Buddha's incredible love for nature. He was always soft-spoken, never raising his voice to prevent stirring up the great land in deep slumber. Not only did he keep his voice down, he also deliberately walked slowly to avoid hurting the Earth by running and jumping on it. The Earth allows us to survive and grow, so how can we injure it? He also would not casually throw trash on the ground. Why? Because he didn't want to pollute the beautiful Earth.

The Buddha also asked his monastics to observe a retreat period from mid-April to mid-July because when it was the monsoon season in India, during which monastics were supposed to stay indoors and curtail their traveling. Why? One reason is that with all the rain, bugs and animals would go out and the monks and nuns didn't want to squash and kill the little creatures. It was preferred to retreat and coexist with life.

To protect Brazil and a few other tropical rainforests, the United Nations gave annual subsidies to ban logging. This was both to protect human lives, and to protect the Earth. The farsighted wisdom of the United Nations reflected that people living on this planet are able to coexist with their surrounding environment.

In Taiwan and throughout much of Asia there is a Buddhist tradition of purchasing animals from butchers and pet stores and setting them free into the wild, thus saving them from a terrible fate. Over time, however, many people have only paid attention to the ritual aspect of this tradition without any consideration for the lives they are supposed to be saving. When these attempts to save living beings are thoughtless, it can actually doom them to death.

Suppose someone thinks, "Tomorrow is my eightieth birthday, and I want to free some animals to make good karma. Get me a fish so I can release it!" Such a person may go out and get a fish in a little plastic bag and take their time finding a lake, pond, or ocean to release it into. By the time they get around to it the fish is dead! People have even gone as far as South America to purchase piranhas and all types of poisonous snakes to release to the wild. You can't take an animal out of its natural habitat, take it somewhere around the world, release it into the wild, and expect everything to be fine.

Rather than holding old traditions in ways that don't apply to modern society, we must keep the spirit of the action and adapt it to our modern conditions. Why not put effort into protecting the life that exists in nature rather than "releasing life" in a way that will likely lead to death? Rather than releasing things into the wild, we need to give nature a chance to live. We need to give people a chance to live. To save a life is worth far more merit than building a new monument. Let's first concentrate on preserving the life we have around us.

> Rather than holding old traditions in ways that don't apply to modern society, we must keep the spirit of the action and adapt it to our modern conditions.

Loving nature is loving life, and loving life is part of loving oneself. We are integrally related to the Earth, to all of nature, and to all existence. If you constantly trap animals, the animals will disappear. If you recklessly chop down trees, the air will lose balance and fresh water levels will decrease. If you don't take care of plants, they'll wilt.

For all of us to coexist we need mutual love and care. Without love and without cherishing our families, it's equivalent to not having a family. If we don't hold any love for the rest of society, how can we hope to face it when any disorder emerges?

If all humanity really makes the effort to know and understand society, beginning with the family and continuing outward, we can learn to coexist peacefully. We need to cherish and value the good things that others possess. We must always carry a pleasant attitude. When we see another's skyscraper, we can't let jealousy arise within us. Instead we should not worry, for if it rains we can stand under a neighbor's roof. When I see you buy a television, I can think about coming for a quick peek and enjoying it with you. The space between heaven and earth is teeming with the energy of life; we should absorb it so that it becomes a part of us. To develop our own life force, we must coexist with nature.

> The space between heaven and earth is teeming with the energy of life, we should absorb it so that it becomes part of our own. To develop our own life force, we must coexist with nature.

Part II

The Cycle of
Birth and Death

The cycle of birth and death treats everyone equally: birth and death are universal and certain for all beings. No matter what era a person is born in, and no matter their wealth or social status, death comes to us all. There are people so intoxicated with life that they loathe the very thought of death, and there are others who would commit suicide in the face of a little difficulty. These are the extremes, but overall, birth and death are simply like the relationship between being awake and sleeping. When you fall asleep, it's a little like being dead, whereas waking up is like being born again.

Birth and death are like two sides of a coin. After death, there is birth, and when you are born, you are sure to die. However, there is a phrase that states, "Birth is not truly birth, and death is not truly death." Because it's all actually just one continuing process, we should not worry much over the fleeting appearance of birth and death.

When clothing, houses, or machines are old and worn out, they are replaced with the new. This is something we can feel happy about. Death is like moving into a new body. So the idea of death doesn't have to be feared or pushed away. Why should we have to use this body until it's old, worn out, stiff, and ill? That can be painful, right?

Biologists have said that human cells constantly metabolize in order to maintain a healthy life. So it is obvious that as human beings, we never stop changing. The "I" of yesterday is not the "I" of today. The "I" of today is not the "I" of tomorrow. As human beings, we must pass through thousands upon thousands of "life and death" moments as we grow and mature.

> The "I" of yesterday is not the "I" of today. The "I" of today is not the "I" of tomorrow.

There are many ways to understand the cycle of birth and death. When we see someone in a very deep sleep, we may say they are "dead to the world," but their heart still continues to beat. And as night turns to day, the body comes to life again, in a sense, continuing the cycle of birth and death. Similarly, sorrow and other emotions have their own "birth and death" as they arise and cease. Today's sorrow should not be carried into tomorrow, nor should it be passed onto others. Let your sorrow literally "pass away" at the end of the day.

According to Buddhism, there are two types of "birth and death": that which is experienced by sentient beings and that which is experienced by bodhisattvas and arhats. Ordinary sentient beings only experience fragments of the cycle of birth and death. We only see process, but cannot see the whole. Each time a sentient being is reborn, their appearance and lifespan differs according to their karma. As one life ends, the next begins, without much awareness of what is going on.

Bodhisattvas and arhats experience the cycle of birth and death differently. Such beings have incredible self-cultivation and have compassion for all beings. They see the cycle of birth and death functioning in all things: the rise and fall of virtues, understanding, perception, and awakening. Bodhisattvas and arhats are different from sentient beings, for while their minds are still part of the cycle of birth and death, their bodies are unrestrained by it, and can be manifested as they wish.

Things like impermanence and birth and death are universal truths, and as such, they are always present in all things, everywhere, all the time. Because such truths are assured and equally present among all things, we should learn to accept them as a part of life.

Suffering arises and ceases like the cycle of birth and death. Our thoughts and our knowledge arises and ceases as well. Birth and death are like two sides of a coin, similar to how the *Treatise on the Awakening of Faith in Mahayana* describes the "one mind that opens two doors." The "door of suchness" transcends birth and death, whereas the "door of arising and ceasing" leads to birth and death. Things like impermanence and birth and death are universal truths, and as such, they are always present in all things, everywhere, all the time. Because such truths are assured and equally present among all things, we should learn to accept them as a part of life. By accepting them, we can reduce or even eliminate the mental stress that comes from the cycle of birth and death.

It is similar to falling ill; if we know how to befriend our illness, we won't get frustrated. As long as you can look life and death in the face and accept their existence, fear will cease. It's easy to give up fame and wealth, but it's difficult to give up the fear of death.

During the time of the Buddha there was a woman whose son died and she was inundated with grief. She went to solicit the Buddha's help: "Lord Buddha, as powerful as you are, would you please revive my son?"

The Buddha told her, "There is only one way to revive your son. If you can find some 'auspicious grass,' I can use it to save him."

She asked, "What is 'auspicious grass?'"

The Buddha said, "Knock on the door of every household and ask if anyone in the family has ever died. If you find a family without death, the grass they grow is considered auspicious grass."

"Knock on the door of every household and ask if anyone in the family has ever died. If you find a family without death, the grass they grow is considered auspicious grass."

37

So the woman went and asked everywhere she could, "Has anybody ever died in your family?" But whose family has never suffered a death? She did not find the auspicious grass, but in the end she realized that death visits every family. Having accepted the universality of life and death, she finally came to peace with her son's passing.

CLOSE CALLS WITH DEATH

When facing death, it is best to avoid any concerns, such as not wanting to die, losing your wealth, or fear of the unknown.

At my age, it's hard not to start thinking about death. I have been practicing how to face death when it comes. Over the years, I've let go of all greed and desire in this secular world. I realize that nothing is mine. Everything occurs within the framework of karma. When facing death, it is best to avoid any concerns, such as not wanting to die, losing your wealth, or fear of the unknown. By letting go of any such concerns, I gradually prepare myself for what could be after death.

My life has already had numerous close calls with death. While playing on the ice of a frozen river one winter when I was seven or eight years old, I thought I saw an egg laid by a goose or a duck. Actually it was a breakage in the ice and when I reached it, I naturally fell in. There is no reasonable way I could have been saved, but I got out without knowing how. When I arrived home, my family saw that I was nearly frozen. It seems that when your final day has not come, you cannot die even if you want to.

I grew up in China during a time of great turmoil. Once, the police force of the Communist Party arrested me, claiming that I was an agent of the Nationalist Party and that I would be executed. I had been

But, I still belonged to no party. I was merely a monk.

a monk since I was 12, so I actually had little knowledge of the political situation at the time. When I arrived in Taiwan, the Nationalists also wanted to execute me, and called me a Communist spy. But, I still belonged to no party. I was merely a monk. I remember it was during the time of the "White Terror" in Taiwan, a period of great social unrest when many people were wrongfully imprisoned and killed. Master Cihang and I were both arrested and jailed for more than twenty days. It was only with the help of a few devoted Buddhists with strong military and political connections that we were finally bailed out.

On one occasion, I was bound with ropes by the Communist's police force that was preparing me to be sent to the execution ground; I thought I was about to be shot to death. It was about 2 or 3 o'clock in the afternoon and the sun was shining brightly. As I was walking, though not afraid, I felt the sun was dim because I was thinking that to die at the age of 22 is really a great pity; my parents didn't know about it, nor did my master. I felt nervous, realizing the impermanence of life, and that life lasts for but a single breath. It was only afterwards that I learned the incident was merely an interrogation.

After I came to Taiwan, I resided in a temple. Every day, I'd take a cart and travel seven kilometers to purchase rice and vegetables. When there was less to buy, I'd ride a bicycle to do the shopping. But at that time, I wasn't very good at riding a bicycle, and on a narrow path one day, I suddenly saw two students coming my way.

"Ahhh," I shouted. I thought I was going to hit them. What should I do? Immediately, I blurted out: "Get out of my way!"

I was upside-down in the air, feeling like the whole world was turning. I told myself that I would die for sure.

But it was too late. Distracted by the students, I lost control of my bicycle and went straight into a three-story deep, stone-filled irrigation ditch. I was upside-down in the air, feeling like the whole world was turning. I told myself that I would die for sure.

40

A few minutes later, I looked around and saw that Hell still had earth, grass, trees, and stones, just like the ones on Earth. Then I touched my ears. I grabbed my muscles: "Wow, this is actually still my old self! I'm not dead!"

I looked over and saw the bicycle was completely destroyed. But I was quite intact! I was too reluctant to give up the bike, so I bundled it all together and shouldered the wreckage back home to sell later. "Normally I rode on the bicycle," I wrote in my journal that night, "but today the bicycle rode on me."

In yet another case many years ago, I was in a hospital getting a check-up when the doctor found that I could have had an incurable condition. Not being able to tell me that I didn't have long to live, he asked me, "Are monks afraid of death?"

This is really hard to answer skillfully. If I said, "Yes," then he'd think I was useless as a monk. But if I said, "No," it would sound like a poor argument. Even ants would give up anything to stay alive, how can human beings not be afraid of death? Therefore, I responded, "Death is not as fearful as the pain from it."

If one cannot bear the pain, even a hero can become a coward in the face of death: not a pretty sight to watch. Pain is far

Pain is far more difficult to experience than death. Even the pains of emotional sorrow, the feelings of being bullied, and loss of self-esteem are all be more difficult to bear than death itself.

more difficult to experience than death. Even the pains of emotional sorrow, the feelings of being bullied, and loss of self-esteem are all more difficult to bear than death itself.

We should not let the past make us miserable. Even if the past is negative, it can still nourish us, develop us, and provide us with support and valuable experience to learn from.

Therefore, when faced with death, we should calmly accept it without fear.

A few decades ago, there were a few seniors who wanted to live at Fo Guang Shan with the thought that, after they passed away, there would be monastics to pray for them, so we constructed a Senior Citizens Home at Fo Guang Shan. Those elders went on to live there for decades. Many even lived past one hundred years of age. Why did they live so long? Because they were no longer afraid of death, and when the fear of death is gone our life expectancy expands.

People should be prepared for death, whether their own death or the death of others. When their elderly pass away suddenly, many families are flustered and confused, not knowing what to do. This is because they were not prepared.

Prepare clothes for cold days when you are in a warm season; save your money when you have extra. Schedule death into daily life so you won't be flustered when it actually comes. Life and death are never predictable. Some people are still very healthy after eighty or ninety years of age; others may die suddenly while still young. There's a Chinese expression, "When Death wants you to die at midnight, you cannot live to see the morning."

> **Prepare clothes for cold days when you are in a warm season; save your money when you have extra. Schedule death into daily life so you won't be flustered when it actually comes.**

Death is unpredictable no matter how old you are, how healthy, how wealthy, or how intelligent. There is a Buddhist saying: "Do not wait until you are old to learn the Way. There are many young people buried in tombs." Death does not wait for us. So put it on your schedule. Whatever you want to do, do it without delay. Be prepared, don't live in fear, and start doing what really matters for yourself and in your relationships with others.

⚮ ⚮ ⚮

THE PRECIOUSNESS OF LIFE

During my thirty-eight years at Fo Guang Shan Monastery, the most difficult thing I encountered was trying to expand it. When I tried to buy land from people, most did not dare to sell. They'd often use the excuse, "We'll discuss that later." I feel such reasoning is unskillful, for whatever needs to be done should be done sooner rather than later. Sometimes there is no later in life. If we all wait until later, we might have to wait until the next life. After all, the future is not guaranteed to anyone.

If we all wait until later, we might have to wait until the next life. After all, the future is not guaranteed to anyone.

In my own life, as long as it's something I should do, I do it without hesitation. If someone helps me, I return their hospitality as soon as possible; if someone needs my help, I give assistance as soon as possible. We can't always say "later." If one wants to be a filial son or daughter, don't wait until your parents are gone.

We can see that although humans live to be a hundred years old, we still need to treat life like just one day and make the best of it. Don't give up life easily, and don't be afraid of it either. Death is natural.

To encourage people to use their life to its full potential I launched the "million education sponsors" campaign so that people could foster education around the world and cultivate good karma through generosity at the same time. Every day, when you say a nice word to someone, you gain merit; when you smile at someone, you gain merit; when you have a good thought, you gain more merit. Continue to gain merit for yourselves, and spread the contributions, benefits, help, and affinity to others.

According to Buddhism, there are four kinds of life. Some life is born in the womb, like human beings, pigs, horses, oxen, and sheep. Some life hatches from eggs, like chickens, ducks, birds, and tortoises. Some life is born from moisture, like frogs and mosquitoes. Some life is born of transformation, such as supernatural and heavenly beings.

Life can also be categorized according to habitat. Some life lives in the mountains, like tigers, wolves, and wild animals. Some forms of life live largely in the air, like birds. Some life also lives buried in the earth, like worms. Life is full of wonder. Some living things have two feet, some have four, and some have many feet. Life also comes in all shades of different colors.

No matter what kind of life, beings differ both in the manner of birth and the process of death. Some die of old age. Some die when they have used up all their merit. In a way, people meeting the end of their life is similar to using up their savings in the bank. When the proper conditions are no longer present, life breaks apart, just as a married couple seeks a divorce when the conditions keeping them together are no longer present.

In Buddhism we often analyze things in terms of the four great elements of earth, water, fire and wind. Take a house for example: Steel and cement are hard, making up the earth element. Stirring up cement and painting the walls need the water element. Bending the reinforcing bars and welding require the fire element. The architecture calls for air ventilation, making up the wind element.

Human beings are the same: Our bones are the earth element; our urine and sweat are the water element; the heat from our body is the fire element; and our breathing is the wind element. Human life requires each of these four elements. But when they are not in sync, we will suffer from illnesses, such as bone spurs, edema, high fevers, and difficulty in breathing. When such conditions are right, things come together and the body is healthy, and when conditions cease, things break apart and there

> When such conditions are right, things come together and the body is healthy, and when conditions cease, things break apart and there is illness.

is illness. In the same way, when the right conditions are present, the Buddha enters the world, and when those conditions are no longer present, the Buddha enters *nirvana.*

Someone can sacrifice his life for an ideology, for a cause, or for saving a person's life. This kind of heroic spirit deserves praise. Some die in accidents, which cannot be controlled by human beings. Death is not fearsome, but what is fearful is that many times things happen out of the blue.

There are many suicides nowadays. In some countries, suicide is a crime, just as homicide is, and committing suicide does not help solve any real problems. It is selfish conduct for the one who commits suicide to leave sorrow and chaos for family and friends to deal with. To commit suicide is not just selfish, it is also cowardly. If one does not fear death, then he is dauntless with everything else. Even if he is deeply in debt, it will be all right, for he can pay the debts in the long run. As long as there is life, there is hope.

Someone may say: "I am ill; my love life is unpleasant, so I want to kill myself." This is a silly attitude—there are billions of people on earth. Surely there are other people out there for you. Why throw one's life away because of a single person?

Whenever unexpected things happen, you should stay calm. Even when you are quarreling, remind yourself that you need to keep a clear head. If someone says, "Let's stop arguing. We can start talking again in five minutes," maybe in those five minutes the idea of committing suicide will change.

> **Those who can live worry-free can also die worry-free.**

My advice is this: it is better to live than to die. Life can be painful, but killing yourself does not solve the problem. Those who can live worry-free can also die worry-free.

The way that modern people view death is progressing. A few generations ago in China people used to use the expression *shishi* (逝世), "leave the world," to talk about death. These days it is much more common for people to say *wangsheng* (往生), "go to the next life." The expression "go to the next life" implies that nothing has truly ended, and that we are just moving to another place. That being said, if we regard death as traveling to another world, or going to heaven or the Pure Land, "death" can be a happy occurrence.

However, people are filled with paradoxes. Many Buddhists chant *"namo amitofo,"* meaning, "I take refuge in Amitabha Buddha." Amitabha Buddha resides in a realm far from our own called a "Pure Land," where all who are born there live with such bliss that they can easily practice the Dharma. When Buddhists take refuge in Amitabha Buddha, they are expressing a wish to be reborn in his Pure Land. Now, if you were to ask someone why they chant Amitabha Buddha's name, they might tell you, "I want Amitabha Buddha to welcome me into his Western Pure Land of Ultimate Bliss." But if Amitabha Buddha were to actually appear before this person, he or she would be very surprised and say, "Amitabha, I do not want to go to the Pure Land yet! My son is not married yet, my elder daughter hasn't found herself a husband, and my younger daughter still needs my help." Many people are confused about what they really want in any given moment.

> Many people are confused about what they really want in any given moment.

For example, there is a story about a young man whose father passed away. In Chinese culture, Buddhists often hold chanting services to pray for their relatives to have a fortunate rebirth. The young man wanted his deceased father to attain a fortunate rebirth, so he went to a monk, asking him to chant. "Master, my father is gone. How much will it cost for you to chant for him?"

The monk murmured, "Hmm, how much should it be? Thirty dollars for the Amitabha Sutra and the Diamond Sutra."

"This is too much", said the young man.

So the monk asked the young man, "How much do you think it should be?"

"Why not give me a discount? Say, twenty percent? How about twenty-four dollars?"

The monk replied, "Alright. I will conduct a chanting service for twenty-four dollars."

When the chanting was over, the monk started praying, "Oh, departed father! Now I am releasing you. Hurry and go to the Eastern Pure Land!"

The son pulled at the monk's robes, "Wait! Wait! Others all go to Amitabha's Western Pure Land, why do you send my father to the Eastern Pure Land?"

The monk said, "Going west costs thirty dollars. You wanted a twenty-four dollar service, so I can only send him to the east."

"Oh, just to save six dollars, my father had to go east instead of to the west. This won't do. Master, please pray again, and send my father to the Western Pure Land."

So the monk prayed a second time. "Oh, departed father! Now your son has changed his mind and he gave six dollars more, so I pray again to send you to the west."

Then, the father suddenly jumped out of the coffin, pointed at his son, and scolded him, "How could you? Just to save six dollars, you made me go to the Eastern Pure Land and then all the way to the Western Pure Land. Now I'm exhausted!"

Humans all desire to have peace when alive and to be free when dead. But a Buddhist sutra states that when humans die, it's like a turtle shedding his shell, a snake molting its skin, or a prisoner having his handcuffs and shackles removed.

In the sutras, it says that Amitabha Buddha's Pure Land is ten trillion "Buddha lands" away from our world. One "Buddha land" is said to be the size of three thousand of our solar systems. Scientists can build a rocket that will land on the moon, but they will never be able to take us to the Pure Land. Going to the Pure Land requires chanting the name of Amitabha, powerful virtuous vows, and mental concentration. The speed of the mind is faster than electricity and light. When you think about Los Angles, London, or New York, your mind is there immediately. So when a person dies and goes to the Western Pure Land, as soon as death occurs on this side, life happens on the other side. Distance is not an issue. One thought can travel across three thousand solar systems in a flash.

When an elder passes away, don't think he is gone. Although the body no longer moves, the consciousness may well be talking to us. But since the spiritual world is formless, we cannot physically hear it. So when we pay homage to our ancestors,

51

we should act as if they are there. Unless our ancestor has been reborn and taken a new form, when we miss or commemorate them, they should know.

Many years ago, I read a book that described life after death. It said there had been a traffic accident in which four people all died. Observers asked each other, "How did this car get hit like this? How did all the people die?"

One of the spirits who died in the accident tried to tell the crowd, "I know what happened in the accident." But those passing by couldn't see or hear him.

Later, the spirit became angry: "I was at the scene! I have first-hand information! I know all about what happened. Why won't you listen when I offer to tell you?"

Life and death look different, but they may actually be very similar. One question that we could ask is, if there is such a thing as a heaven and a hell, where are they? Sometimes I like to answer that question by saying, "Heaven is in heaven, and hell is in hell."

> If there is such a thing as a heaven and a hell, where are they? Sometimes I like to answer that question by saying, "Heaven is in heaven, and hell is in hell."

What does that mean? Simply, heaven is where there is joy and hell is where there is suffering. In essence, heaven and hell both exist in the human world. Those people leading happy lives with homes and cars are in heaven. Those who are mercilessly killed or suffer from cold and hunger can feel like they are in hell. Sometimes, one person can commute between hell and heaven several times in a single day. One virtuous thought raises you to heaven; one malicious thought sends you to hell. Therefore, if you ask "Where are hell and heaven?" they can be found right in our hearts and minds.

> If you ask "Where are hell and heaven?" they can be found right in our hearts and minds.

Where are life and death? Life and death do not dwell inside the body, nor do they exist between breaths. Life and death go hand in hand. Birth is destined for death; after death there will be another life. There once was a Chan master who saw one family with a newborn son. He commented: "Poor thing! Another dead person added to this family."

"Why did you have to curse the baby?" one family member asked.

"Once a person is born he is destined to die, isn't that right?" When death comes a person is released from this life, obtains a new body, and enters another cycle of rebirth. For the issue of life and death, no matter what view you hold, it is important that you both accept life and be prepared for death.

Dying with Dignity

We often read the words "died of natural causes" in obituaries, this is a very dignified way to die. In traditional Chinese families, sometimes the body of the deceased is held behind curtains so that people cannot see it, and the body itself is draped in cloth covered in *dharanis*, special passages from Buddhist sutras. This is also done so that the person can have a dignified death. If the family and relatives cry their hearts out and experience great affliction, it can make the deceased worried and irritated, and thus unable to die with dignity.

Just like sleep, death can be very serene. Death is very natural, as natural as a lamp going out when all the oil is used up. It is possible for one to die without disease, with a mind that is unconfused, without attachment, and without worries or concerns. Such a person can die with a smile on their face. Even if a person does not want to die, such a thing is not possible. If a person does not want to be reborn, it is just as impossible.

So how can we transcend death? As ordinary human beings, we do not know where we come from when we are born and we do not know where we go when we die. If we become

54

arhats, an advanced spiritual practitioner who is liberated from the cycle of birth and death, we can then truly understand birth and death. An *arhat* is one who loathes the cycle of birth and death and sees birth and death as heavy karma that is beyond his control. Because of this he turns away and abandons the cycle of birth and death.

A bodhisattva, however, is one who works to alleviate the suffering of all sentient beings. Bodhisattvas have transcended birth and death, and no longer fear the cycle of birth and death. They see birth and death as the same. They can transform within the cycle of birth and death to be as they wish. Bodhisattvas

> A bodhisattva, however, is one who works to alleviate the suffering of all sentient beings.

have complete freedom, but they remain in the world to help others become free as well. This state is called *"nirvana* with remainder."

Concerning the dignity of death, I feel that being able to die with dignity has much to do with the power of karma, and the power of vows. If our negative karma unexpectedly comes to fruition, then we will have an unpleasant death. That is why we should rely on the power of vows, and vow to be reborn in the Pure Land. In addition, we should vow to bring peace to the world, to bring joy to the people, to have no pains in our body, and to die with no disease. Making wholesome vows allows us to succeed.

There is a thought-provoking metaphorical story in the Buddhist sutras. A rich man married four women and the fourth one, who was young and beautiful, was his favorite. When the rich man was dying, thinking that on the road in the underworld he'd be very lonely with no company, he yielded to his emotions and asked his youngest wife, "You are my most beloved wife. Will you die with me?"

The fourth wife turned pale and said, "What!? How can I die with you? We love when we are alive. How can there be love after death? I don't want to die."

The rich man was quite disappointed, but thought, "It's okay. I am also very fond of my third wife." So he asked the third wife, "Will you die with me?"

She said, "Of course not! I am still young. After you die, I can still remarry, so I can't die with you."

The rich man could do nothing but go to the second wife. "I have treated you well. Will you die with me?"

The second wife said, "No! If I do, there will be no one taking care of this household. As husband and wife, we get along well. I can take care of your funeral, send you to a desolate place outside the town and then bid you farewell. But I can't die with you."

He thought in dismay of how he had ignored his first wife and felt that he had no hope with her. Contrary to his expectation, the first wife was very willing to follow his request. "We women follow the man we marry, no matter what. I am your wife; of course I'll die with you." The rich man was so surprised.

After a long distance, one will know a horse's stamina. After a long time, one will see a person's heart. The fourth wife is a metaphor for our body. It needs makeup and protection every day so it won't be hurt. But once it is dead it won't pay any attention to us anymore.

> After a long distance, one will know a horse's stamina. After a long time, one will see a person's heart.

Who or what is the third wife? It is gold and silver, money and stocks. Money is made for others. It will not follow you.

The second wife is like our family and relatives who occasionally will think of you and help you but cannot die with you. They can only burn some incense at your tomb or send you to your cemetery.

The first wife is a metaphor for the mind, for when death comes, nothing can be taken with us except for our karma, borne in the mind. From this you can see that this world is very practical. Practical as it is, we can still reverse it in that we love the first wife because she lives and dies with the master. In essence, we should cultivate our behavior and our mind. Once our mind is cultivated, we can build merit and virtue. These are what carry us on through life and death.

I've mentioned previously that birth and death are alike but, that being said, human beings still view them differently. They'd rather bitterly endure in this world than be buried in the earth. It is very good to remain alive because life is valuable. To sustain our lives, many of us suffer through countless hardships. Therefore, we should cherish life even more.

There are many people who loathe this world, but those who leave the world and become monastics feel aversion to worldliness in a different way than laypeople. Those who become monastics inherently wish to turn away from worldly things. But for those who remain in the world, it is fitting and proper to want wealth, love, and a steady career. As long as one has a good heart and wishes to benefit others, the wealthier the better, the more love between a couple the better, the more dutiful the children the better, and the closer linked the family is the better!

Buddhism does not advocate that people should have no love at all or should not have family. Buddhism has always cared very much about people. In this world, people should maintain worldly laws. Couples should love each other and lovingly raise their children. Children are not something to be endured, they are boundless potential. They will return all that we invest in them in the future, and even if they do not, it is okay because we should focus on what seeds we plant rather than on what we harvest. Money is not always bad; it can be earned ethically, helping you to achieve your career, and realize your dreams and aspirations.

A suicidal person will have difficulty weathering tough situations. He may take things too hard simply because of a word from a family member or something caused by a family member, or because of debt, out of love, or just because of being unlucky. Suppose at a time like this there is a friend who can come to his aid, saying something or doing something to help change his mind so he'd turn his attention away from suicide; or with a person who failed in the business world, encouraging him to set up a street stand to at least sustain the family. Do not overemphasize your status. "I used to be a general manager; I used to be a president..." Professions like cab driving, and rickshaw pulling are also sacred. What is wrong with making wealth by physical labor? What is the need to commit suicide? Killing oneself is a behavior of the weak; it is running away from problems, leaving them for the entire family.

Rather than limiting yourself, think outside the box; release yourself from the box or you will never be at ease. Those who find themselves often wanting to commit suicide should begin to develop an optimistic attitude, live an active life, treat others nicely, take care of others, cultivate good affinity, and then make these activities consistent life-habits. Consequently, when the thought of committing suicide pops up again, there will be good karma to help you out of the predicament.

Do you think that I cling to my body now that I've reached the age of eighty? Maybe I did when I was sixty or seventy. Why? At that time I was still building Fo Guang Shan Monastery. I would think, "Look at these trees I've planted and these houses I've built. If I were to die now right after they have been completed, what a pity it would be."

We live in an always-developing society. Even if I were to build everything again, we would still continue to develop for over one hundred years.

But I no longer have that perspective. After all, we live in an always-developing society.

Even if I were to build everything again, we would still continue to develop for over one hundred years. At the age I am right now, with regards to life and death, I just proceed as conditions arise.

The most important precept in Buddhism is not to kill. Whether it is killing others, killing oneself, taking joy in others beings killed, or giving orders to kill, all of these are breaking the precept, and all of these are wrong. Suicide is harmful in and of itself. Do not think that people can hang themselves or overdose on medication and that, once life is over, all troubles will be settled and gone.

There is a story in the Buddhist sutras about an ugly girl that no one loved. As such, she resented her parents. Seeing others enjoy their youth and having fun and falling in love with each other, she felt lonely. Feeling worthless, she threw herself into a river to drown herself.

Just at that moment, an old monk came along and saved her. The old monk said: "The girl who just tried to commit suicide is now dead. What I have saved is a reborn life. You killed your old self because you only thought about your own problems. But from this day forward, do not only think about yourself. Think about others. Serve others. Devote your life to others."

> "The girl who just tried to commit suicide is now dead. What I have saved is a reborn life."

Hearing this, the little girl seemed to have been awakened. Ever since then, she helped other people everywhere she went. With the openness of her heart, her temperament gradually changed and she even became physically more attractive. Later, she met a promising young man who was attracted not only to her outer beauty, but to her virtues and her kindness. In the end, they happily married each other. So we can see even physical changes are influenced by changing one's thought patterns.

Life After Death

Many sages and Buddhas have provided guidance on the question of what happens after death. Death is like the water flowing out of a broken cup. Even though the water leaves the confines of the cup, the water itself will not disappear. The implication is that the body is dead and it cannot be revived. But the water of life will still flow elsewhere in the process of rebirth. Just as the rolling water

> **Death is like the water flowing out of a broken cup. Even though the water leaves the confines of the cup, the water itself will not disappear.**

in the ocean turns and churns, and water cycles through stages of evaporation and rain, beings continue their existence in new forms.

The fire of life continues burning, just like prayer beads connected by a string so they won't scatter. Humans have karma and karma is our thread. Whether wholesome karma or unwholesome karma, it unceasingly links all different periods of our life together.

Life, in another example, is like graduating from one school and moving on to a higher level; it also can be compared to changing one's career—saying goodbye to one profession and changing to another.

It is said in the Buddhist sutras that after you die you can see a long tunnel. If you see a white, bright tunnel, it means you are to be delivered to some pleasant higher realm; if you see a dark tunnel, maybe you are to be delivered to some lower realm. For some people, after death, migrating from this life to the other life takes seven days; for others, it takes forty-nine days. So some go quickly and some go slowly, depending on their past karma.

During the process of migrating to another life, there is an intermediate state. This means after death, the body is gone and only the spirit remains.

According to one Buddhist sutra, an individual's rebirth can be determined by feeling the location of heat on the body after death. If there is warmth in the head, it indicates that the person will be reborn as a sage; if there is warmth in the eyes, it indicates going to a heavenly realm; if there is warmth in the chest, it means rebirth in the human realm; warmth in the belly designates the hungry ghost realm; if there is warmth in the knees, one will be reborn as an animal; if there is warmth in the soles of the feet, it's a fall into hell.

The speed of going to the other life is very fast, especially for those who have great power of vows or strong karma. It is even faster for those who have immense virtues or those who have vast evils. Normally, the time it takes to venture on into another realm follows a pattern of sevens. It is what we call the first seven or the first two sevens. "Seven" is an amazing number. In Christianity, every seven days there is worship. Likewise, in Buddhism, there are meditation retreats and Amitabha Buddha chanting services that last for seven days, as well as forty-nine day (7 x 7) seclusion periods. Seven is also closely linked to life and death. It is said that a person is open to moving on from the intermediate state to their next life every seven days. This is why Chinese memorial services are held every seven days after a death in the family for a period of seven weeks.

Life after death is a miraculous experience to me. When I was little, every year on my birthday, I felt dizzy and sleepy the whole day through. I didn't know why at that time, but that stopped after I became a monk. When I think back on that time, I wonder if my dizziness was because it was not long after I had died in my previous life, and my grieving family was still holding memorials for me.

It is not easy for a family to deal with death. There are several forms of hospice and end-of-life care, but this kind of attention need not wait until the final moment.

All people grow old, and all people become ill, and it is at times like these that they need attention the most. A patient suffering from illness needs some extra care, some extra condolence. Caring for people in their time of need is an art. If someone is suffering from a cold and you go and visit, you can't say,

> All people grow old, and all people become ill, and it is at times like these that they need attention the most.

"Getting a cold is very dangerous. You should be careful! I have a friend who passed away half a year ago just because he got a cold." You will only scare them! When speaking to patients we need to say things that are propitious and joyful.

Besides speaking with them, giving gifts to the elderly is also an art in itself. Taking my own life as an example, I have been diabetic for forty years and during these years many friends and fellow Buddhists have visited me out of kindness. They bought many candies and confections for me, but this wasn't really proper to do. Candies don't help a diabetic have a better life.

There are proper ways to communicate with people. When we console the elderly, we can carry smiles but we must be careful to not laugh too loud or be insincerely and over-the-top cheerful. If we do, some people might think, "Why should you laugh so happily when I am ill?" As you can see, we must take the middle way between extremes of going too far and not going far enough.

In ancient Chinese culture, when someone in the family passed away, only direct offspring were allowed to be present. In modern times things are different since people's networks have expanded so much. According to Buddhism, when people pass away, others should pray for them. By the time someone passes away his heart may have stopped beating but their consciousness may still be with them. It is helpful if others come to their aid and ask the Buddha to support them.

There is a tradition we have that says the body should not be moved within the first eight hours after death, but I do not think it is necessary to observe this practice. The eight hour rule may have originated from the previous agricultural age. In those days, when a parent passed away, their children, old enough to be working outside, couldn't come back in time. Consequently, the time to move the body was postponed. When someone dies, the living should not weep over the body.

When people weep or cry, the consciousness will not be as willing to move on. They will then become greedy for life. If someone has just passed away, you must be careful in moving them. The consciousness can still have some sensation linked to the body and touching them can cause great pain, leading to their resentment or hatred. That's why it became a rule to leave some time before moving the dead body. Nowadays, hospitals usually send the body to the mortuary as soon as possible because they do not want the dead body to lie in the bed for eight hours.

> When someone dies, the living should not weep over the body. When people weep or cry, the consciousness will not be as willing to move on.

When someone seems like they may be approaching death, we can put a Buddha statue where they can see it. It can also be soothing for people to hear chanting, but it is not necessary to have people come to chant, as playing recordings of chanting can help to do the work. People present should be composed and serene. In general, do not allow the deceased to fear, become confused, attached, worried, or hateful. Moreover, in a "tranquil ward," the temperature, the air-conditioning should also be properly adjusted. If the consciousness is unconfused and unattached, others can help it to make vows and chant for its benefit.

> A wise person will treat death gracefully, with no worries, no attachments, and no fears.

Dying people can help themselves by also preparing a gift to the right person, and making sure that everything has been taken good care of. If things are not taken good care of, there will be problems later on. A wise person will treat death gracefully, with no worries, no attachments, and no fears. The body is like a suitcase. When I need it, I lift it up; when I do not need it, I put it down. Now I do not need my body any more, I will put it down and get a new one.

The biggest obstacle in passing away is whether you can let things go. It's like walking down a road; if you do not complete the first step how can you take the second step? Letting things go can help one to be worry free.

FREEDOM FROM BIRTH AND DEATH

Buddhists will often say that the goal of Buddhism is to be free from the cycle of birth and death, but what does that mean? Most people don't know anything about being "free from birth and death." If someone asks you why you practice meditation, what do you say? Would you say it is to be "free from

68

birth and death"? What about if someone asks you why you are a Buddhist? Would you say, "So I can be free from birth and death"? Are there any people who are free from birth and death? Can you find one?

There actually are many people in this world who are free from birth and death. The process can be divided into five stages:

1. When I am content with life and do not fear death, I am free from birth and death.

2. When during life I have extra energy to help others and leave much virtue to others after I am gone, I am free from birth and death.

3. When faced with death, if I still keep my heart upright, keep my mind from greed and I vow to return to this world again, then I am free from birth and death.

4. When I no longer fall into the lower realms, and auspicious signs and the Buddha land manifest before me, then I am free from birth and death.

5. When I am in the Pure Land, no longer subject to rebirth, but manifest on a lotus seat where I cultivate bit by bit

until I return to the world again riding on my vows, I am free from birth and death.

True Buddhism is simple and easy to implement, so we can benefit from it and continue its practice in our everyday lives.

It is important that we not make any of the Buddhist doctrines seem too miraculous, mysterious, or impractical. True Buddhism is simple and easy to implement, so we can benefit from it and continue its practice in our everyday lives.

Life is the essence. The cycle of birth and death is our form. Everyday living is our function. Essence, form, and function are all integrated as one. If we can treat life and death as one, take control of life, and not bring regrets to our coffin, then death is like the succession of the seasons; the beauty of the autumn wind blowing foliage off trees. In this way, we can be free and at ease. How natural birth and death are! Death is nothing to fear.

Part III

Learning
How To Live

M ost of us have been in this life for decades now, so one may begin to ask, who could not yet understand *how* to live? But in order to know how to live, we must first master how to learn, because the process of living is in itself a non-stop process of learning.

When we are born, we first need to learn how to suckle, how to walk, and even how to be loved. Later, we need to learn how to read and how to make friends. After we grow up, we begin to learn new skills, like how to respect our teachers and honor truth. Even as we grow into old age, we are still learning. Our lives are a series of such learning processes.

I have a disciple who received her PhD from Yale University before happily returning to the monastery. When she returned, she showed her diploma to me and said, "Master, look, I earned my PhD—now what?"

When she was still in school, I remember people around me always applauded when she returned during winter or summer breaks and said, "Look, our pre-PhD returns!" She could finally hold the fruits of her labor in her hands. I just told her, "Now it's time to learn to live."

It's not easy to live a wholesome life. Many people talk about their daily rigors, the difficulties of getting along with others, and the obstacles to maintaining a moral course in life. It is precisely because of those difficulties, that we must work equally hard in learning how to live a truly good life, and this chapter will examine numerous ways to bring such will to fruition.

※ ※ ※

LEARN TO ADMIT YOUR FAULTS

One of the biggest weaknesses in today's society is that we have developed the habit of not saying we are sorry. Once we grow up and rise in status and knowledge, apologizing becomes harder and harder. But human beings are not perfect sages and we all make mistakes. Being able to correct our mistakes is a virtue in itself. This ability to amend our actions is what allows us to make progress.

> Human beings are not perfect sages and we all make mistakes. Being able to correct our mistakes is a virtue in itself. This ability to amend our actions is what allows us to make progress.

It is important that we know when we cause harm to others, and that we want to make amends. Some ask, "Would the Buddha scold people?" Actually the answer is yes, but always with creativity and tact. One quality that the Buddha criticized in his disciples often was shamelessness. People with some sense of humility can easily say, "I wasn't thinking straight and was so bad in how I treated you. I'm really sorry and want to make it up to you in any way that I can."

What is the benefit of admitting your faults? Saying that you are sorry can sometimes make all the difference. When a parent is staring down their child, about to burst into anger at some misdeeds, a simple apology said at the right time makes all the difference in the world.

I often tell a story about two families. The husband in the first family would always argue with his family, while the second family was very harmonious. One day, the husband in the quarrelsome family asked the husband of the harmonious family what his secret was.

"Why don't you fight in your family?" he asked.

"In my family, each of us thinks that we are the 'bad guy.' That's why we don't fight."

The husband of the harmonious family replied, "The reason you fight in your family is that both of you think you are the 'good guy.' On the contrary, in my family, each of us thinks that we are the 'bad guy.' That's why we don't fight."

The quarrelsome husband was utterly confused, "That doesn't make any sense. Why is it that the 'good guys' fight with one another while the 'bad guys' live in peace?"

The harmonious husband answered, "Since both of you think you are the 'good one,' you always think you are right. This is why you argue."

"Suppose someone in your family put a cup at the edge of the table and it was then broken by someone else," the harmonious husband continued, "If you both think you are the 'good guy,' the one who broke the cup will not want to be blamed for what happened, and will shout, 'Who put the cup there?' The one who placed the cup at the edge will shout back, 'Why did you knock it over?' It is hard to avoid argument if you both always believe that you are right."

"However, if the same situation happened in my family, the result would be different. The person who accidentally broke the cup would say, 'I'm sorry. I accidentally broke the cup.' And the one who set the cup down will say, 'It's not your fault. I should never have placed it at the edge of the table.' Our family members have no trouble owning up to their mistakes, so there is no need to quarrel."

In order to live in a community, the first and foremost thing is learning how to apologize. When small trifles never become big issues, families and friendships are built unhindered. If you really want to bicker, limit yourself to one sentence and force yourself to stop. Otherwise it will endlessly go back and forth

Sages of the past earned their revered status in part because they had no trouble saying, "I'm sorry."

There is no shame in parents admitting faults to their kids or teachers acknowledging mistakes to students. Sages of the past earned their revered status in part because they had no trouble saying, "I'm sorry."

I used to run Pumen Middle School in Kaohsiung. One of our senior teachers there, a father of many children, used to say, "It's hard to raise kids. They always complain about the food you try to cook for them."

I told him, "Don't lecture your kids about what a great parent you are. You have to learn to admit your mistakes and stay humble."

He took my advice and when his children complained how "yucky" the food was again, he said, "Kids, I'm truly sorry. I am not much of a father, because I can't make more money and can't afford to buy better food and clothes for you."

After hearing this, his children vied with each other to say, "Dad, you are the best. The food is delicious!" Today, his kids are no longer picky. Admitting your faults will not cause you to "lose" anything. You can actually appear more confident and open-minded.

About two thousand years ago, there was a king named Asoka. He was of a wicked nature and bad temper. Through conquest, King Asoka was able to unify the entire Indian subcontinent. But whenever he visited the defeated countries, even though all the people came to welcome him, he could feel that the eyes of the people were full of hate. He defeated those countries, but he failed to conquer the people's hearts. It was not a true victory. Later, after becoming a follower of the Buddha's teachings, King Asoka became a kind and humane ruler. As a result, when he visited those countries again, all the people happily welcomed him with sincere conviction.

> Even though all the people came to welcome him, he could feel that the eyes of the people were full of hate. He defeated those countries, but he failed to conquer the people's hearts. It was not a true victory.

Asoka realized that real victory lay not in conquest by force, but in conquest through benevolence. King Asoka went on to be known as one of India's wisest and most virtuous leaders.

Every year, King Asoka would hold a banquet and invite the most eminent monastics from throughout his kingdom. During these banquets the king himself would offer food and bow to each monastic, one by one.

One year, he was surprised to see a very young novice monk in the procession. He thought, "Today I have gathered the most venerated monastics in my kingdom, but what is this little novice doing here? I am king, how can I bow to a child in public?"

Asoka feared that if he did not bow, he would be criticized for breaching etiquette, but he also feared that to bow to a child was beneath the dignity of a monarch. Unsure of what to do, Asoka lead the young novice to a quiet place away from the crowd and whispered, "As you know, I am king—I will bow to you, but do not tell anyone."

The novice then completely surprised the great king. He laid his alms bowl on the ground, and shrunk himself so small that he could dance around the edge of the bowl and jump inside. King Asoka could only stare wide-eyed with his mouth agape. He knew that only the most highly cultivated monastics could display such abilities. The little novice then returned to normal size, leaned closer to King Asoka, and whispered, "Your Majesty, I did this only for you, so do not tell anyone!" King Asoka realized his arrogance and learned not to judge anyone by their appearance.

To do or say something wrong is not so terrible. What is important is that we correct our mistakes. The great sages of the past do not tell us to live perfectly, but instead say, "There is no greater benevolence than admitting one's transgressions and correcting one's mistakes."

In Buddhism, the monks need to uphold two hundred and fifty precepts, while the nuns order has three hundred and forty-eight precepts, and lay Buddhists take five precepts, and sometimes the "Bodhisattva precepts." It is a major commitment to expect someone to take all five precepts at one time. Instead, we can ask that people take some precepts and uphold them to the best of their abilities.

Inevitably, people's observance of the precepts is imperfect, but it is personal ethical training. Never beat yourself up for mistakes. Just sincerely admit your faults and commit to improve. While we can all apologize for our wrongdoing, it is not so easy to apologize for faults that arise due to wrong views.

> Never beat yourself up for mistakes. Just sincerely admit your faults and commit to improve.

Wrong views are those that fundamentally oppose Buddhist principles, and as such can lead us to do serious harm.

Some see the Buddhist precepts as restrictive, and thus refuse to follow them. Such people only see the precepts as a list of things that they can and can't do, and what is and is not allowed. Quite to the contrary, the precepts actually allow us to be free.

Consider the five precepts. One who follows them does not harm the life, property, or reputation of others. Not only does that mean one will not commit any crimes, but following the five precepts also shows a respect for the freedom of others.

The first precept, to refrain from killing, refers to all forms of killing, even rats and cockroaches. However, there is a difference in severity between killing a cockroach and killing a human. If someone kills a cockroach, feeling sincerely sorry for the action can atone for it, whereas if a monastic were to kill a human, they would be expelled from the monastic community, as it is a much more serious offense.

The difference lies in the attitude. One who upholds the precepts would admit the mistake, while others may not.

People who uphold the precepts always remain vigilant against violations of the precepts. If someone who upholds the precepts kills a mouse, he would instantly think, "This is wrong. I killed a mouse." In the same situation, another person might say, "Nice kill!"or boast to others, "I killed a mouse today, and I hit it right on." The difference lies in the attitude. One who upholds the precepts would admit the mistake, while others may not.

The fifth precept is to refrain from consuming intoxicants such as alcohol. During one speaking engagement, I surprised a lot of people when I said that if a Buddhist were to drink alcohol the wrongdoing is of a lesser nature than a non-Buddhist. Why? A Buddhist who wants to drink will generally not drink when others are around, and likely not drink excessively. Plus he may lament, "How disgraceful. I am a Buddhist and still drinking. This is not right." Admitting his wrongdoing, the effect will be lighter.

However, someone who is not trying to uphold the precepts will generally urge others to drink as well, get very drunk themselves, and end up doing harm to themselves and others. It is always beneficial to be aware of our transgressions, great or small, and constantly work to improve ourselves.

> It is always beneficial to be aware of our transgressions, great or small, and constantly work to improve ourselves.

People are very good at making excuses. For example, someone who is late to a meeting might say, "A phone call came in when I was ready to step out" or "A friend suddenly visited me" or "It was raining and the traffic was heavy." Never admitting one's faults is hardly a laudable quality. But, if we can learn instead to admit when we do something wrong, our world can shift from one of conflict and competition to one of peace and cooperation.

LEARN TO BE FLEXIBLE

If someone is too tough or stubborn, one can say that they have a cold heart, or even a heart made of stone. But consider this: our teeth may be hard and rigid, but they will each fall out as we get older. On the other hand, the tongue more or less retains its form even after we die. In general, things can sustain themselves more easily if they are flexible, but tend to be damaged if they are too rigid.

Once the Buddha's Light International Association was providing disaster relief following a typhoon. I saw that the brick houses collapsed, but thatched cottages remained intact. I then realized flexibility could help withstand strong wind and resist external forces.

One time, I assembled a group of practitioners who had been on a six month retreat in the meditation hall and asked, "Have any of you made any progress, or wish to share your meditation experience?"

It is difficult to attain awakening, but after this six month experience with meditation, most people said, "My heart has become softer." I was very glad to hear such comments. After practicing meditation for a while, one will realize there is no need to argue over petty things, no need to be rigid, and no need to compare with others. One's heart will become softer and one's mind will become broader, just as the bough of a tree with ripened fruit bends, or how the branches of a willow tree are beautiful due to their soft and gentle swing.

Truly, the greatest progress you can make in your cultivation is the softening of the heart. If we regulate the breath, relax the body, and train the mind through meditation, we can gradually rein in and pacify our monkey-like minds and horse-like wills. Our days will be happier and our lives will be longer.

Master Hanshan once said: "The strings of a hard crossbow always break first; the blades of a sharp knife chip more easily." The same rule can be applied to live our lives. We should honor harmony and congruence in our relationships.

As soon as a fist thrusts forward, it loses power. When the fist remains in, one's power is sustained. We should never be impulsive in our actions or complain about little things that don't really matter. Impatience and stubbornness lead us far too easily toward grief and suffering. For example, there was once a premier named Feng Dao in China with a very short temper. One day, one of his servants purchased a pair of shoes for him which cost eighteen hundred copper coins. His colleague, He Ning bought a similar pair of shoes, so Feng Dao asked, "How much did you pay?"

He Ning raised his foot and said, "Nine hundred."

"What? You only paid nine hundred? I paid twice as much! Bring me the servant who bought these shoes. I want to teach him a good lesson."

He Ning then lifted the other foot slowly and said, "Don't be so upset. This one cost nine hundred too. Together they were eighteen hundred." As you can see, one with an angry temperament is always at a disadvantage.

We all hope that we can have friends who are peaceful and pleasant, but there may be some who say, "These days, if you aren't fierce and relentless, others will take advantage of you."

"The virtuous may be bullied by the wicked, but heaven does not bully them. The wicked may be feared by the virtuous, but heaven does not fear them."

But these kinds of setbacks are temporary. As the Chinese proverb states, "The virtuous may be bullied by the wicked, but heaven does not bully them. The wicked may be feared by the virtuous, but heaven does not fear them." One may win or lose, but in the end, the result depends on you. One cannot rely simply on brute force, instead it is important to focus on the details. Everyone is different, and if we can be flexible and not so rigid, we can accept this.

LEARN TO BE PATIENT

In Buddhism, we talk about a type of patience that is different from ordinary patience. Called *renru* (忍辱) in Chinese, there are three kinds of Buddhist patience: Patience for life, patience for phenomena, and patience for the non-arising of phenomena.

What is Buddhist patience? It has several layers of meaning. In this context, patience does not necessarily refer to refraining from talking back when scolded or "turning the other cheek." First it refers to the ability to recognize, know, and clearly see the patterns of cause and effect, right and wrong, or gain and loss involved in any issue. Next, it involves being able to accept these things just as they are. To accept any situation that arises, good or bad, requires both power and wisdom. Finally, patience also means calmly taking on responsibility when the situation calls for it. This helps us to alleviate conflicts, solve problems, and resolve differences.

> Patience also means calmly taking on responsibility when the situation calls for it. This helps us to alleviate conflicts, solve problems, and resolve differences.

For example, when his dad came back from work, a little boy was excited and said "Dad, you've returned! Now let me ride on your back like a horse." Although the father was tired and not looking forward to it, he still smiled and said, "Okay, hurry up and get on my back!" The father was willing to graciously accept because his son is so precious to him and he can undertake any responsibilities that relate to his son. However, the response would have been quite different if this request had come from someone else. If we treat everyone around us like they are our family, we can always have the patience to perform good deeds.

> To live a happy life, to be a person of indomitable spirit, and to get along with others, patience is an invaluable virtue to cultivate.

Patience can be cultivated, and there are many benefits to doing so. For example, by cultivating patience for life, we can better understand the profound causes and conditions that are at play in all of our relationships. For example, you can have patience for your parents through more deeply understanding all that they have done and sacrificed for you. Your spouse can appreciate how much you understand his or her perspective and you can mutually grow in affection. To live a happy life, to be a person of indomitable spirit, and to get along with others, patience is an invaluable virtue to cultivate.

People know they should be more tolerant, should change their short temper, and should not argue over trifling issues.

But it is hard to let go of that one sentence somebody said to you or that one action they did. For example, many of the people engaged in lawsuits are actually only doing it because they could not control their anger, not because the issue is truly a serious one. Maybe they can endure other hardships, like hunger, coldness, or heat, but they cannot restrain their anger. An old Chinese proverb states, "Swallow your anger then the wind is fair and the sea calm; back up a step and the sea becomes wider and the sky expands."

There is an interesting story about patience and Buddha statues. These days, the Buddha images found in temples are made from a variety of different materials: some are carved out of wood, some are cast in concrete, some are made of stone, and some are simply paintings on paper. But in the old days, most Buddha images were bronze statues.

Once, long ago, someone came to a Buddhist temple to pay homage to the Buddha. Each time he bowed before the Buddha statue, he would knock on the big bronze bell. The big bronze bell was very unhappy, and later complained to the Buddha:

"Even though both of us are cast in bronze, people come to worship you and offer flowers and fruit. I don't get any of that—instead they hit me! It's so unfair. I even hear some of them say, 'Bow to the Buddha without hitting the bell, and the Buddha will not believe your piety well.'"

The Buddha statue replied to the bell, "Big bell, don't feel bad. I remember when the sculptors were trying to make me into a Buddha statue. If there was a lump around my ear, they would knock me around and beat me. If my nose wasn't smooth enough, they would dig and carve into me. I've been pounded by hammers thousands of times and tempered a hundred more to become a Buddha. That's why people are willing to bow in front of me. But look at you, with just a gentle knock, you complain and moan, 'booong, booong,' without any patience. How could people worship you?"

Patience does not mean suffering. Patience is strength, it is our life-force. Patience is the wisdom and understanding that recognizes the causes and conditions of a situation.

In current management science, such as managing money, there is usually no serious criminal violation except for embezzlement, considering money does not talk. When dealing with other properties, such as moving a table from here to there, the table cannot fight back. It is at the mercy of your will. It is very easy to manage money and material possessions, but it's another story to manage people, since people might not be obedient. However, if you truly understand interpersonal relationships, managing people is not difficult either. Honestly, what is far more difficult than managing people is managing one's own mind.

What is far more difficult than managing people is managing one's own mind.

For example, there was a general on a battlefield and no one dared to disobey his command. But when the general went back home, as a henpecked husband, he might be too scared to move upon hearing his shrewish wife's "lion roar." Therefore, it is easier to manage with an established law and authority system. But what if you encounter someone who is unreasonable and does not follow the rules? All we can do in this case is be patient. One party must be willing to compromise in order to quell the heat of the debate. Any problem becomes easier to solve with the wisdom of patience.

Learn to Communicate

Communication is an art. Although modernity has many advanced scientific inventions, graciousness and other virtues are still indispensable for humanity. We should learn to respect others, learn to be tolerant, learn to be harmonious, and learn to communicate effectively. Countries should not merely resort to force to resolve problems all the time. Developing more advanced weapons has lead to endless war. Only if international communication becomes smooth, can we have world peace. For example, the healthy relations on either side of the Taiwan Strait rely on better communications.

A smooth communication process requires several essential ingredients: negotiation based on a win-win approach, results that please all parties, mutual respect, equality, and harmony.

But a smooth communication process requires several essential ingredients: negotiation based on a win-win approach, results that please all parties, mutual respect, equality, and harmony. An agreement can always be reached if everyone maintains a humble attitude.

There is a story about a family in which the son wanted to marry a girl, but his mother strongly disagreed. She said, "If you marry her, don't come back home anymore."

But the couple's love was too strong. The son chose to marry the girl and moved out of his mother's house. More than ten years passed. The son never returned home after his marriage and the mother held a grudge, thinking, "Well, it's fine if you never return. I don't even care whether or not you're dead."

After some time, a friend finally persuaded the elderly mother, "You can't carry on like this! Even the Berlin Wall came down. After over ten years, you must tear down this wall in your own heart and let them come back."

The mother broke down upon hearing her friend's plea, and saw the truth in those words. "Wow, it has already been more than ten years. Who am I to harbor such enmity?" Through the friend's mediation, the mother finally asked her son and daughter-in-law to move back in to her house. For such reconciliation to take place, one party always has to begin with a concession.

Why were the mother and daughter-in-law so incompatible? The man had the dual role of being a son and a husband. When the mother and wife both want him all to themselves, it is certainly difficult for them to develop any rapport with each other. Such a situation is also difficult for the son caught in the middle. He has his filial relationship to his mother and his desire to be with his wife pulling at either side of him.

One day, the son came up with a brilliant idea. He told his mother: "Mom, my wife is no good, but we're married, so I can't help it. I need your support. If you could just be nice to her for the next six months, I will tell her to leave after that."

"A half year would be no problem," his mother replied.

The son then separately spoke with his wife, "I apologize for dragging you back into this house with my mother. If you can just be nice to her for the next six months, we can move out after that." His wife agreed.

Both the mother and wife tried their best to fulfill their promise to the son, treating each other as nice as they could for the next six months. The relationship between them steadily improved, and the mother and daughter-in-law grew steadily closer to each other. The mom finally told her son, "You can't let your wife go. Put up with her and let her stay." The wife also finally told her husband, "We really mustn't move out!"

Our words have the power to both anger people and bring them joy. That's why Buddhism tells us to avoid any harmful speech. Whenever we are communicating with friends or relatives, it's important to get along. But what do I do if someone is unkind to me? Imagine if I took the position that, every time someone rebuked me, I would talk back, and every time I was slandered, I would return the same to them. This policy of "an eye for an eye" will never end.

When people criticize us, we should say good things about them. Eventually, it will come around, and they will hear what we say about them. The slander will eventually slow to a halt, the rift mended, and the gap eliminated.

My grandmother was a vegetarian and a devoted Buddhist practitioner, but her daughter-in-law, my aunt, was an unruly woman. She often performed a "trilogy" consisting of: 1. Crying, 2. Making a scene, and 3. Threatening to hang herself. But, in time, she completely changed her ways. What led to this turn-around?

One day, somebody began telling my grandmother what an awful person her daughter-in-law was. Upon hearing this, my grandmother immediately said, "Stop it. My daughter-in-law treats me very well."

My grandmother then began to list all of her daughter-in-law's positive traits. The daughter-in-law just happened to walk in the back door and overhear the conversation. She felt overwhelmed by the kindness of the words she heard and ashamed at her previous attitude. Compassion ultimately has the power to subdue any hatred.

Poor communication often stems from attachment. There once was a parapet that was white on one side and black on the other. Two warriors shot arrows through either side of it. One of them commented on the white parapet they just shot at. The other countered and said the parapet was surely black. Both stuck firmly to their own views, before eventually walking to the other side of the parapet and realizing the truth. Our attachments in life are just like this parapet and our perceptions vary depending on our perspective viewpoints. We should always try to walk in another person's shoes.

We often have some tough issues at Fo Guang Shan that my disciples do not know how to handle. For example, in one instance someone came to me and said, "Master, could you please help?"

"What is the problem?" I asked.

"There is a staff member who always misbehaves himself and gossips. We should dismiss him. Master, can you talk to him please?"

I said, "Okay, let me handle it."

Later, my disciples asked me, "Master, how did you solve this so easily?"

I do not have any super powers. I do not have three heads or six arms, but I know how to praise others. I told the staff member, "How long have you been here? Everyone talks about your hard work and great contributions. But we have to make some adjustments because of various reasons. We will offer you two months of severance pay. Please do come back to tell me after you locate a job somewhere else." Most people will readily accept such an offer with gratitude.

It is not difficult to have good communication, you just need to offer the other party something to feel good about.

It is not difficult to have good communication, you just need to offer the other party something to feel good about. If both parties can work together as if in a dance—sometimes backing up, sometimes moving forward—everyone can move together in harmony.

In 2008 the "three links" were established across the Taiwan strait which allowed for mail, travel, and trade between mainland China and the island of Taiwan. These reforms were possible due to the sincerity of will from both sides. It was a win-win situation in which both local economies can benefit. It's a good thing when everyone can benefit and prosper by working together.

Of course, good communication skills are based on numerous conditions: being knowledgeable, citing the proper instances, familiarity with history, ability to give accurate quotations, speaking succinctly and to the point, maintaining a sense of humor, and being sincere. These are the basic conditions for good communication, but if one's ego is too big, one always talks about their own opinion, never makes concessions, and creates thick communication barriers. We must always keep in mind that there are others besides "me."

One year I was giving teachings on the *Diamond Sutra* in Los Angeles, when my mother, who was in her 90s at that time, was listening to me backstage. After I finished, she criticized me, "You do not know how to properly explain the sutra!"

I asked my mother, "Which part was not clear?"

"I understood when you said there is no notion of self, but how can there be no notion of others?" What she meant was that we must always keep sentient beings in mind and that it would be wrong to have "no notion of others." Of course, the phrase "no notion of self, no notion of others, no notion of sentient beings, and no notion of longevity" that appears in the *Diamond Sutra* has another, specialized meaning, but my mother's comments allowed me to look at it from another perspective.

Someone who suffers from vision problems may see aberrations in their vision which are very real to them, but would never show up if the object being observed were examined under a microscope. We form attachments when we have delusions about the world. The Buddha taught the "four means of embracing" in the sutras, and they can be very helpful for communication. The four means of embracing are: giving, kind words, altruism, and empathy. These four methods together can attract and draw people in or even help in creating friendships and partnerships. Kind words, smiles, and offers of help can all bring happiness to others.

Empathy is exemplified in a mother feeding her baby. When a mother feeds her baby, the baby can feel the love of its mother showing that the two are the same. Altruism lies in doing good deeds for others, granting them convenience, and providing them space when they need it. When it comes to kind words, you can quickly amass three to five hundred kind words if you even write just a few kinds words a day. Speaking kind words does not necessarily mean continuously saying, "I love you." That might work between a husband and wife, but saying that to some other people might be rather offensive. We should speak the decent and appropriate words for every context in any given situation.

Some young monastics are not so skilled at complimenting lay people. They only think to say, "You have a generous heart." Isn't there anything else to say? They could say, "You really have right view; you're very hardworking, very decent; you really carry an elegant style in your speech; you have a very harmonious family; you're public-spirited."

The Honorary President of the Buddha's Light International Association, Wu Poh-Hsiung promoted the "Three Benevolent Acts" campaign with the aim of getting people to purify their karma of body, speech, and mind. The "Three Benevolent Acts" are doing good deeds with the body, speaking kind words with the mouth, and having benevolent thoughts in one's mind. This campaign successfully improved the moral fabric of the local society. Regularly speaking kind words and praising people will neither cost money nor take much effort.

However, we should be careful to not praise others too casually. People might think its sarcastic and become unhappy. Some people have a short temper. If you praise them for being "gentle and soft", they will think they are being accused by your "praise." No matter what you say or what you do, you must make sure people can accept it. Once you follow these guidelines, you can communicate with much greater ease.

Learn to Let Go

Letting go does not mean losing something. Actually, letting go allows us to be free. We should pick things up when it is time to pick them up, and let things go when it is time to let go. Consider a suitcase: much of the time it lies on the ground. We only pick it up when we are about to travel. It is not necessary to hold a suitcase in your hand all the time, wherever you go. Wouldn't that be excessive?

> Letting go allows us to be free. We should pick things up when it is time to pick them up, and let things go when it is time to let go.

Once a man came to visit the Buddha bringing two pots of flowers as offerings. When the man stepped into the Buddha's quarters, the Buddha said to him, "Put it down."

The man set down one of the pots of flowers. The Buddha said again, "Put it down."

The man set down the second pot of flowers. The Buddha said a third time, "Put it down."

The visitor asked, "I've put down both pots of flowers, what is it that you want me to put down?"

The Buddha replied, "Put down your views, put down your attachments, and put down your suspicion."

If we do not know how to let go and put things down, even if we have a good reputation, wealth, high status, love, and so on, those things will ultimately only serve to provide more attachment and stress.

We can see executives, chairmen, and managers play with stocks every day. Are they not under pressure? The truth is many of them cannot sleep at ease like ordinary people. Their whole moods are tied to the daily stock market, exchange rates, and other such things. They live with constant attachments. Many wealthy people cannot live as carefree as the rest of us. They sit in high buildings and large mansions every day, dealing with checks. Although the number on the check might be millions or even tens of millions, a check is nothing but a piece of paper. In contrast, common people have many pieces of paper—they just have $1 or $5 written on it with beautiful illustrations. That is far more interesting.

It is not necessarily a blessing to be rich. There was once a young couple. When they went back to their small makeshift hut from work, one would play music and the other would sing along. A very rich chairman was living in a mansion adjacent to their hut. One day the chairman said: "Those two are really carefree. They still cheerfully sing and play musical instruments even though they live in a hut. I'm always frustrated, even though I get to come home to this beautiful estate every day!"

The chairman's secretary said, "Mister chairman, if you don't want the stress, why don't you give the young couple some of your money? Say, a million dollars? Let them worry about it instead."

The chairman said, "What? A million dollars? Isn't that making things a little too easy for them?"

The secretary replied, "Well, it doesn't hurt to give it a try." So the chairman decided to really give the couple a million dollars of his own money.

The couple received the money and were elated. But then they began to worry, "Where should we put it? In a drawer? No, that wouldn't be safe. What if a thief breaks in? How about in the pillows? No, then the pillows would be too big and uncomfortable to sleep on."

The couple stayed up all night worrying about what to do with the money. Finally, at dawn they began to think, "We were wrong. We feel duped. This money has only caused us trouble."

So the couple took the million dollars back to the chairman saying, "We want to return these afflictions to you. We no longer want your million dollars."

In the past, I was hurt and slandered by many people, and I just let it go; I have also been praised by numerous people, but I still do not let that effect me. However, I once received praise from a teacher that I appreciated so much, I would like to share his words with you.

I was the president of a Buddhist seminary at that time. A teacher said, "Our president can take serious matters so easily." I still remember that time: there were so many things to do, and so many bridges to cross to promote the Buddha's teachings. I also needed to attend morning and evening chanting, and attend to all the visitors who were coming and going. But I was the venerable master and the president, so no matter how busy I was, I couldn't tense up and let others see me rush here and there. I should appear calm and at ease. So I carried a relaxed expression as if nothing had happened, even if I was extremely busy. I felt that a heavy workload could be accomplished with the greatest of ease.

Everyone in society shoulders many kinds of pressures, whether at work or at home. It is critical to learn to let go and work through them with ease, for with an attitude that is calm, confident, and worry-free, we can overcome any difficulties that arise.

CELE) CELE) CELE)

LEARN TO INSPIRE AND BE INSPIRED

Do you feel inspired when you see people help each other? Not everyone is. Some people may look at a generous donation and say, "Donating such a small amount of money is nothing extraordinary for such a rich person." When other people suffer from disasters and pain like the many people killed in the South Asian tsunami and earthquakes, don't you feel for them? Doesn't it make you think, "What would it be like if I were in that position?"

> "If I were the person who is suffering, wouldn't I hope for the compassion of others?"

People often say to me that it is hard to be compassionate. How can we be more compassionate to others? We can begin by placing ourselves in others' shoes. Think, "If I were the person who is suffering, wouldn't I hope for the compassion of others?"

Inspiration comes from our interaction with others. When I see people do good deeds, I feel moved. When I see people suffering, I feel compassion. What is important is that, in our actions, we try to touch the hearts of others and feel that sense of purity ourselves.

Take a moment and think about all the kind words you can say to move other people, and all the good deeds that can affect others. Life will lose its meaning if what we do and what we speak cannot touch others.

> Life will lose its meaning if what we do and what we speak cannot touch others.

It is a beautiful thing to touch people's hearts, as is being moved by others. We could say that all the touching moments put together is what makes this world a beautiful place. Why is it that when seeing the plot unfold during certain movies or performances, we cannot help but to cry? This is because we feel a connection to the people on screen. Some people are even moved to tears when hearing the pure and tranquil sounds of Buddhist chanting.

Allow me to relate one such touching story:

At a given meditation hall there were a great number of students. One day, something was stolen from the meditation hall, and the thief was caught. It happened to be one of the practitioners.

Everybody was talking about the matter, "The meditation hall is a sacred place. Who would dare to steal there?"

"Let's report this to the head of the meditation hall! He'll dismiss him."

So the other practitioners presented their case before the Chan master who was the head of the meditation hall, but the Chan master just nodded and said, "Oh." The thief was not punished.

Later, another item went missing, and the same person was caught stealing. One of the other practitioners brought the thief before the Chan master and said, "Dismiss him!"

Again, the Chan master simply nodded and said, "Oh," but still did not expel the thief. So the thief kept stealing, and at last everyone in the meditation hall came to the Chan master with an ultimatum: "If you do not expel the thief, the rest of us are going to leave!"

So the Chan master said, "You all can leave now. He will stay."

"You will let us all leave and allow the thief to stay? You're crazy!"

"If not even the meditation hall can accommodate him, I really doubt he could find any other place in this world."

The Chan master replied, "You are all normal people who can make a living wherever you go. But he is a thief, so how can he lead a normal life in society? If not even the meditation hall can accommodate him, I really doubt he could find any other place in this world." Although it was difficult for the thief to break his vicious habit, upon hearing the Chan master's words, he burst into tears and made up his mind, "I promise, I will no longer steal!" Later, he became an outstanding Chan practitioner.

In another story, a thief came to a Buddhist temple to steal while a Chan master was meditating. The thief thought the master was dozing off, so he rummaged all over the place to take what he wanted. Finally, he was satisfied and ready to leave. Right after he stepped over the threshold, the Chan master suddenly yelled, "Stop!"

The thief was scared out of his mind. The master said, "You took my things and my money, and you just leave like this without saying 'thanks?'"

Upon hearing this, the thief quickly said, "thank you" and ran away.

Later, the thief was caught by the police. He confessed that he once stole money from the Chan master. So the police took him to the Chan master and asked, "Did this man ever steal your money?"

"No, he didn't."

"Venerable, this thief has confessed. He even told us the day he stole from you."

With a smile, the Chan master responded, "But that was not stealing. I gave the money to him. If you don't believe me, you can ask him if he thanked me when he left."

The thief's heart was so touched when he heard what the master said that after he finished his prison sentence, he returned to the Chan master and became a monk. Later, he himself became a renowned Chan master. We should all try to help others by touching their hearts.

When Fo Guang Shan Monastery organizes large-scale events, there are always monastics from other traditions standing outside, soliciting donations. In the old days, Chinese monastics used to stand still when soliciting donations, no matter how much was offered. But now some monastics will walk directly up to people to ask for donations. This is not very good since, in Buddhism, we promote upright, pure, and solemn behavior—approaching people for money in this way is surely not proper.

I once heard some Buddhist followers say something very reasonable: "Real Buddhists don't worry about imposter monks." An imposter monk who was soliciting donations outside the monastery once said, "Fo Guang Shan can hold such a large-scale activity, and there are so many people who support you. You have such a big piece of the pie, why can't we have the leftovers?" Most people would think that if one group spends so much time to organize an event, there is really no need to share the fruits of that labor, but when I heard that comment, I thought, "It's true, we should leave something for others, instead of taking all the donations for ourselves."

In the newspaper one day, I read a story about a child who saw the fruits his mother bought, and wanted to leave some for the family members who had not yet returned. But he didn't know how to write "Daddy," "Brother," or "Sister." So he tried to carve their faces on the fruits.

When his mother saw that her son had dug into all the fruits, she was very angry and gave the child a hard spanking because she thought it was a prank. When asked why he did so, the child said while crying, "Mom, I was afraid someone would eat the fruits before daddy, sister, and brother come back. So I carved daddy's face on the fruit for daddy, I carved sister's face on the fruit for sister, and I carved brother's face on the fruit for brother." The mother was very touched and regretted having spanked her son.

In Japan there was an eminent monastic named Hakuin who had a follower who was a businessman. This business-man's daughter became pregnant after an affair with a young man. The businessman was furious and lambasted his daughter. The girl thought, "With such a blazing temper, my father will certainly kill my boyfriend," so the girl asked her boyfriend to run away.

The businessman interrogated his daughter about the iden-tity of the father. The girl thought Master Hakuin was the one her father respected the most and it would make things easier if she said that Master Hakuin was the father of her child. So she told her father that she had the child with Master Hakuin.

For the businessman it was as if a mountain had crumbled and the earth had split open. He couldn't believe that Master Hakuin, a man he worshipped like the Buddha, was actually even worse than an animal. He rushed into the temple and gave Master Hakuin an indiscriminate beating. Master Hakuin didn't defend himself, even when his head was bruised and bleeding. After his daughter gave birth, the businessman took the baby directly to Master Hakuin and said. "Here is the root of your troubles. Take it!"

A monk suddenly had a baby. You could imagine how hard this was for Master Hakuin. He had to beg for milk every day even if it was rainy or windy. Rumors spread that Master Hakuin was an old monk of careless virtue and the baby was his illegitimate son. Some children even threw stones at him, calling him a bad monk.

A couple of months passed, and the young man who fled came back. After the girl told him what had happened, he felt very guilty and determined to turn himself in to the businessman. Although the businessman was furious as a father, he was glad to know the truth as a disciple of Master Hakuin.

The whole family traveled to the temple, bowed before Master Hakuin and sincerely apologized for everything that had taken place, Master Hakuin simply returned the baby without any complaint.

LEARN TO SURVIVE

Society must possess certain defensive powers to survive, like natural disaster prevention processes, policies and procedures. People should also bear in mind that while vigilance should always be taken against criminals, we should never harbor ill intent towards anyone.

What qualities should we learn to help us survive? Qualities like diligence, politeness, optimism, positive thinking, interconnectedness, helpfulness, and being resistant to pressure.

If we learn to treat other people well, other people will treat us well in return. Learn to work hard, and it will certainly bear fruit. Learn compassion and there will be rewards. I feel that I have been well-off throughout my life because I do

If we learn to treat other people well, other people will treat us well in return. Learn to work hard, and it will certainly bear fruit.

not care if I lack something, and I am happy to see others have things that I do not.

Over the past several decades since I came to Taiwan, there have been numerous occasions in which I've been harassed and hurt by others, but I never think to retaliate or hold a grudge against them. Once, I received an invitation from a foreign country for a visit. Back then, opportunities for international travel were rare, so I was very happy.

"Wow! I'll be able to go abroad," I thought. I was in Kaohsiung, Taiwan at that time and I had to head several hours north to Taipei to attend the meeting that would decide if I would be allowed to travel. I took the night train and arrived in Taipei around 7am in the morning. It was 9am sharp when I got to the meeting venue, and the meeting had just begun.

The host of the meeting looked at me and said, "What are you doing here? We've decided you cannot go. You can go back now."

Since the host was an elder monastic, I merely said: "I'm sorry. I am not qualified to attend the meeting. I'll leave now."

I felt awful on the return trip. I thought, "If this was the case, why was I asked to attend this meeting in the first place?" Examples like this are too numerous to enumerate. I just tolerated them and endured the humiliation. Enduring each experience is like the cycle of birth and death. Only after thousands of trials through such cycles can you finally escape and survive.

The most important thing in life is to survive. In order to survive, we must maintain good health. This is not only for our own benefit, but also helps put the minds of our friends and family at ease. Maintaining good health is a way to

Maintaining good health is a way to show filial piety, and allow one's family to be harmonious.

show filial piety, and allow one's family to be harmonious. In order to survive, we also need to work hard, be active and have good manners so that we can be a part of society. In order to survive, we must effectively manage money, handle relationships, take care of our daily tasks, be mindful of our personal conduct, and communicate well with others. A country can only be secure when its actions accord with the will of the people; likewise, for the individual, we survive through our acceptance of those around us.

To survive, you must be accepted by others. For this reason, the causes and conditions for coexistence are very important. If your actions cannot be accepted by others, there will certainly be barriers to your survival.

How can we live our lives at ease? Everyone expects things to turn out as they wish. But what about helping others to do what they want and achieve their goals? Have you improved yourself? To survive in the world, one must acquire others' acceptance, recognition and appreciation. That is how to be free.

LEARN TO BE CLEVER

Are all people clever? There are plenty of people who would proudly proclaim their own cleverness. Others might admit to being a bit slow, but cleverness can always be learned.

> As long as you listen carefully, pay attention, mindfully focus on the ins and outs of the whole matter, and its causes and effects, over time, the clever, resourceful qualities will begin to come naturally.

Some people are born more clever than others, but daily learning is also very important. As long as you listen carefully, pay attention, mindfully focus on the ins and outs of the whole matter, and its causes and effects, over time, the clever, resourceful qualities will begin to come naturally. If you don't listen carefully, handle matters carelessly, assume arrogant positions, and always talk about yourself, then you will never learn.

What does it mean to be clever? Consider the following story:

Once there were two Chan temples that were located near one another. Every morning each temple would send a novice to the market to buy supplies for the temple. The novice from one temple was much smarter than the novice from the other temple and one day these two novices ran into each other on the road. The less clever novice asked the smarter novice, "Hey! Where are you going today?"

The smart novice replied, "I go wherever my legs take me."

The other novice could not think of anything to say in response, so when he returned he told his master what happened. His master said, "You're so stupid! When he says, 'I go wherever my legs take me,' you counter with, 'If your legs cannot move anymore, where do you go?'"

The novice exclaimed, "Oh! That's how it is!" The next day, he ran into the smart novice again and asked, "Where are you going today?"

This time the smart novice responded differently and said, "I go wherever the wind blows."

The novice had no idea how to respond to this answer, so he returned to his master and told him what happened. The master sighed and said, "You're so stupid! When he says, 'go wherever the wind blows,' you counter with, 'If the wind stops blowing, where do you go?'"

The novice replied, "Oh, I see."

On the third day, he ran into the smart novice again, so he asked, "Where are you going today?"

The smart novice replied, "I'm going to the market," and the other novice was once again at a loss for words.

When people reach the end of their resources, they must turn around and change their ways to bring clarity.

The Chan School emphasizes cleverness and acting according to the circumstances. When people reach the end of their resources, they must turn around and change their ways to bring clarity. Without a bit of cleverness, it is not easy to act this way.

It is said that in the early years of the Republic of China, there was an elderly monk named Jingpu, known for his sense of humor. He also often accepted pirates, robbers, and bandits to become monastics. Yet, he himself was never in danger and he possessed very strong leadership skills.

Once, he was giving devotees a tour of the temple. At that time, there was a disciple who could not resist the temptation and brought some beef jerky to the temple. He was eating it in secrecy when, halfway through his snack, he saw Master Jingpu and the devotees coming towards him. In a panic, he dropped the beef jerky to the ground.

When the old monk saw it was beef jerky, from far away he said, "The kohlrabi that you dropped, take it away." One sentence resolved the embarrassing situation.

Later, he took the devotees to visit the meditation hall. Inside, the meditation hall was still with silence, as everyone was meditating. The elderly monk pointed at the people in the meditation hall and humorously said, "These people are under my direction. They all listen to me."

The discipline master inside the meditation hall did not know who was speaking and said, "Who is it that is speaking so loudly!?"

Jingpu turned to the devotees with a smile, and said, "Everyone listens to me, but he is the only one who I listen to."

People should learn to be clever and have a sense of humor.

Besides the eight kinds of learning I have mentioned previously, there are a few other little lessons that are valuable to learn:

1. Live Simply

We must rely on material things to live, but it is important that, when it comes to these material possessions, we learn to be simple and plain.

2. Learn Skills

There are a lot of skills to learn in this life. Many of these skills are essentially for getting by. For example, how to cook rice, prepare a meal, and make tea are all important tasks that both men and women should learn. There is a proverb that says, "Even if your house be full with gold, it shall not equal the one who valuable skills doth hold." Even if you are incredibly rich and wealthy, that money will simply disappear without the skills to make good use of it.

3. Have a Sense of Humor

Language is like perfume. There is an old saying that "Kind words can warm three years of frigid winters." Kind words can bring a great deal of joy. Once the mother of a lady who was over thirty years of age and not yet married came to me and said, "Master, please encourage her to renounce and become a monastic."

I replied, "I cannot do that, how can you tell someone to renounce?"

Instead I asked the young lady, "Miss, why don't you get married?"

She sighed and said, "These days, men do not have any sense of humor." When young women of the past sought a husband, they looked at family status, wealth, health, and education, but apparently now a sense of humor has more importance. All the men out there should take note—money does not necessarily bring happiness, a sense of humor can fill the house with laughter.

4. Embrace the Arts

Art provides beauty, character, and a welcoming atmosphere. Life's greatest task is to come into your own, and find out who you are. In my opinion, art is a critical part of self-discovery, and can help us to find the inspiration we need.

5. Learn to Be in the Background

When dealing with matters, one needs to be well-rounded, modest, and reserved. Just as many Chan stories do not reveal a specific answer or moral, we need to allow leeway for people to think on their own.

6. Work Hard

People at work must learn to be diligent and honest. There is a saying: "To see if a person has ambition or not, look at the way he tends the kitchen fire and sweeps the floor." If anyone acts without diligence and effort, they will not progress. There is value in setting goals because they help in motivating us and pushing us forward.

7. Be Self-Motivated

In order to ascend to great heights we must learn to be optimistic. When people vow to do something, they must be able to summon the will to fulfill their vows. A true vow should not be some vain, momentary promise, it should be something you are able to realize. If we can generate the motivation to fulfill our vows, then we can fly upward, broaden our vision, and develop ourselves so that we may let vitality flow into our lives.

8. Focus the Mind

By focusing the mind on what is at hand, when you are eating you will eat your fill and when you are sleeping you will sleep soundly. When working you will get things done, and when you write your thoughts will be composed. The mind is like a plot of land: it is a field that must be cultivated before you can plant seeds and harvest the crops. As long as you develop it, the ground can give rise to skyscrapers, just as the new land can rise out of the ocean. Each of our hearts is full of many treasures, But we must take the effort to unearth them.

There is so much to learn in life. Even if one lives into old age, it is impossible to learn it all. Many of my disciples have graduate degrees, and when they come and speak to me, I listen attentively so I am always learning along with them. That's why the relationship between the master and disciples is even closer than family. Despite my eighty years of age, there is no generation gap between us. We are part "master-disciple," but mostly just friends. This is what allows me to observe, accept, and examine new things so I can later use them to teach and share with others.

If parents can develop a similar relationship with their children, then children become more than just one's flesh and blood, they can become friends as well. You can share in the joy of their growth and maturation. If teachers can think in this way, they can learn from all their students, and their students will become their peers. If you are a commanding officer, then your troops are not just your troops, but your colleagues and you shoulder responsibility together through good times and bad. Couples in relationships can tolerate and respect each other. If all of our relationships can achieve such a state, how wonderful life becomes!

Life is the essence of our existence. It is not gained nor lost, for life goes on forever: eternal, absolute, limitless, and real. The cycle of birth and death is our form. All manner of phenomena appear in each life, and they are all subject to arising and ceasing, change, and impermanence. How we live is our function. From birth until death the food we eat, the clothes we wear, the places we live, how we travel, the words we say, and the things we do are all activities of the body and mind.

These three—essence, form, and function—go hand in hand. They cannot be separated. Because we live, there is life, and because we have life we exist within the cycle of birth and death. Hence, "understanding life," "the cycle of birth and death," and "learning how to live" can encompass the practice and understanding of Humanistic Buddhism.

Life is valuable. We must make good use of it, so that it's light can shine forth and bring benefit to society. When we make good use of our lives, then we will be peaceful, happy, and content.

Glossary

Amitabha Buddha: The Buddha of boundless light and boundless life. Amitabha is one of the most popular Buddhas for devotion among Mahayana Buddhists. He presides over the Pure Land of Ultimate Bliss.

bodhisattva: While the term can describe a practitioner anywhere on the path to Buddhahood, it usually refers to a class of beings who stand on the very edge of full awakening, but remain in the world to help other beings become awakened.

Buddha: (*Skt.* "awakened one") Though there are many Buddhas, the term typically refers to Sakyamuni Buddha—the historical Buddha, and founder of Buddhism.

Buddha's Light International Association: A lay-oriented Buddhist organization founded by Master Hsing Yun 1991.

Chan (School): A school of Buddhism relying on meditative concentration for the path to liberation. "Chan" is also used to describe the aesthetic and way of life that developed out of this school.

dependent origination: The Buddhist concept that all phenomena arise due to causes and conditions. The central principle that phenomena do not come into existence independently but only as a result of causes and conditions; thus, no phenomena possesses an independent self-nature. This concept is also referred to as interdependence. The twelve factors of dependent origination are ignorance, mental formations, consciousness, name and form, the six sense organs, contact, feeling, craving, clinging, becoming, birth, and aging and death. The term is also sometimes used to specifically refer to the chain of causes that result in suffering, sickness, and death.

dharani: A passage from the Buddhist sutras which is chanted to grant blessings.

Dharma: (Skt. "truth.") Refers to the Buddha's teachings, as well as the truth of the universe. When capitalized, it means the ultimate truth and the teachings of the Buddha. When the Dharma is applied or practiced in life it is referred to as righteousness or virtue. When it appears with a lowercase *d*, it refers to anything that can be thought of, experienced, or named; close in meaning to "phenomena."

emptiness: A Buddhist doctrine that all phenomena have no essence or permanent aspect whatsoever. Consequently, everything that exists in the world is due to dependent origination and has no permanent self or substance.

Fo Guang Shan: Literally, "Buddha's Light Mountain," it is the largest Buddhist order and temple system in Taiwan. Founded in 1967 by Venerable Master Hsing Yun, Fo Guang Shan's main temple and monastery is about thirty-five miles from Kaohsiung.

impermanence. One of the most basic truths taught by the Buddha. It is the concept that all conditioned phenomena will arise, abide, change, and disappear due to causes and conditions.

karma: Literally "action," though much more commonly used to describe the entirety of the Buddhist view of cause and effect. The Buddha stated that the causes, conditions, and rebirth that we encounter in the future are effects of our previous thoughts, words, and deeds.

nirvana: A state of perfect tranquility that is the ultimate goal of Buddhist practice.

precept: Rules of moral conduct taught by the Buddha. The most fundamental set of precepts is the "five precepts," observed by lay and monastic Buddhists alike. They are to refrain from killing, to refrain from stealing, to refrain from sexual mis-conduct, to refrain from lying, and to refrain from consuming intoxicants.

Pure Land: A transcendent realm created through the power of a Buddha's vow to help ease the suffering of living beings, should they choose to be reborn there.

sutra: A Sanskrit word used to describe a variety of religious and non-religious writings, but most commonly used in a Buddhist context to refer to the recorded discourses of the Buddha.

About the Author

Venerable Master Hsing Yun is a Chinese Buddhist monk, author, philanthropist, and founder of the Fo Guang Shan Buddhist Order, which has branches throughout Asia, Europe, Africa, Australia, and the Americas. Ordained at the age of twelve in Jiangsu Province, China, Hsing Yun has spent over seventy years as a Buddhist monk promoting what he calls "Humanistic Buddhism"—Buddhism that meets the needs of people and is integrated into all aspects of daily life.

In 1949, Hsing Yun went to Taiwan and began to nurture the burgeoning Buddhist culture on the island. Early on in his monastic career, he was involved in promoting Buddhism through the written word. He has served as an editor and contributor for many Buddhist magazines and periodicals, authoring the daily columns "Between Ignorance and Enlightenment," "Dharma Words," and "Hsing Yun's Chan Talk." In 1957, he started his own Buddhist magazine, *Awakening the World*, and in 2000, the first daily Buddhist newspaper, the *Merit Times*.

Hsing Yun has authored more than one hundred books on how to bring happiness, peace, compassion and wisdom into daily life. These works include *Being Good, For All Living Beings,* and the *Rabbit's Horn.* He also edited and published the *Fo Guang Encyclopedia,* the most authoritative Buddhist reference work in the Chinese language. His contributions have reached as far as sponsoring Buddhist music and art to creating Buddhist programming for television, radio, and the stage.

Today Master Hsing Yun continues to travel around the world teaching the Dharma. He is also the acting president of Buddha's Light International Association (BLIA), the worldwide lay Buddhist service organization.

About Buddha's Light Pub

Buddha's Light Publishing offers quality translations of classical Buddhist texts as well as works by contemporary Buddhist teachers and scholars. We embrace Humanistic Buddhism, and promote Buddhist writing which is accessible, community-oriented, and relevant to daily life.

Founded in 1996 by Venerable Master Hsing Yun as the Fo Guang Shan International Translation Center, Buddha's Light Publishing seeks to continue Master Hsing Yun's goal of promoting the Buddha's teachings by fostering writing, art, and culture. Learn more by visiting www.blpusa.com.